The H[illegible]ad

What Really Matters in the Age of AI

Paul Iliffe

The Human Thread: What Really Matters in the Age of AI

Published by Staying Human Books
PO Box 7169
Poole, BH15 9EL,
United Kingdom
www.stayinghumanbooks.com

First edition, 2025

While every effort has been made to ensure the accuracy of the information contained in this book, neither the author nor the publisher assumes responsibility for errors, omissions or differing interpretations of the subject matter. This work is provided for informational and educational purposes only.

Research Methodology:
This book was developed through structured human–AI collaboration. All research was conducted with AI assistance under human editorial oversight and judgement. Every factual claim was verified against primary or institutional sources. For further detail, see the Notes section.

Book design by Nadia Iliffe
Illustrations by Paul Iliffe

ISBN 978-1-9192552-1-7

Printed and distributed by independent platforms under agreement with the publisher. For information, permissions or bulk orders:
info@stayinghumanbooks.com

To Nadia, Liam and Shan

Table of Contents

Preface

How This Book Came to Be

The Thread We Carry

Each of us holds a thread that connects us to everyone who came before and everyone who will come after. It's not just DNA - it's humanity's accumulated wisdom, knowledge, stories and hard-won insights about what makes life worth living. During our brief time here, we hold this thread, add our own experiences to it and pass it forward to the next generation. Some parts of the thread grow stronger as we learn more - our understanding of the human mind, our capacity for healing and our ability to create and connect. Other parts fray or get replaced by better knowledge. The thread is constantly evolving, becoming richer but also more complex to understand as human knowledge expands exponentially.

This book began with a growing unease about what's happening right now, in plain sight. The spaces where communities traditionally gathered are vanishing at an alarming rate. In France, cafés declined by nearly 80% between 1960 and 2008 - from 200,000 establishments to 41,500 - a decline that continued through the pandemic years and beyond.[1] The United States saw nearly 16,000 restaurants close in the first half of 2024 alone.[2] Across Britain, 35 chain stores shut every day while eight pubs close each week, up from six just last year.[3] Banks automate what were once human encounters. We scroll through feeds designed to fragment attention rather than build connection.

Each change seems small, even convenient. Taken together, they're quietly reshaping what it means to live as humans together. Technology isn't just changing how we do things - it's changing which things we do at all. The patterns that have sustained human lives for millennia - face-to-face gathering, serendipitous encounters, sustained attention - are being replaced by systems optimised for efficiency and engagement rather than human thriving. These patterns deserve careful transmission precisely because they risk being lost through replacement rather than forgetting. Not just our technologies or scientific knowledge, but the deeper insights about what makes life meaningful, how to love well, how to cooperate under pressure, how to maintain hope in the face of uncertainty.

Why Me

I am not a philosopher or an academic. I am a strategist who has spent over twenty years working for international advertising agencies, finding clarity within complexity - taking technical product briefs and human truths and distilling them into creative ideas that stick. My job was to cut through the information overload and identify what matters.

Like many people, I've watched Artificial Intelligence (AI) capabilities expand with both marvel and concern. But rather than seeing it as a threat to human wisdom, I've come to understand it as a powerful research partner - a tool that can help us explore humanity's accumulated knowledge more thoroughly while keeping human judgement at the centre of what deserves our attention.

A New Kind of Research Partnership

This book distills human wisdom into forty essential themes and practical insights that address the fundamental questions every generation faces. What you're reading emerged from a unique collaboration between human curiosity and machine capability. I provided the questions about what makes life meaningful, the frameworks for organising human experience and the judgement about which insights help people live better. AI provided the research power to explore thousands of sources across disciplines, cultures and centuries.

Every theme in this book followed a systematic process: AI-assisted research explored philosophy, religion, science and culture with every fact verified and every source checked against primary materials. No claim appears without traceable evidence. The Human Thread draws on 500+ sources spanning over 175 academic disciplines - from ancient philosophy to AI safety research, from medieval history to cognitive neuroscience.

Throughout this process, we maintained clear guidelines: humans lead the inquiry while AI assists with research; claims remain modest and when evidence is mixed, we say so; plain language beats academic jargon; and practical wisdom takes priority over theoretical completeness.

Multiple review stages identified weak insights, controversial claims without adequate support or material that was simply repackaging conventional wisdom in new language. Each theme had to reveal something genuinely unexpected - a hidden pattern or fresh lens that makes familiar territory suddenly visible in new ways. Academic insights were translated into metaphors and examples that make sense in ordinary life. Wisdom that can't be easily understood can't be used.

This collaboration revealed unexpected connections I never would have found working alone - historical practices that illuminate modern challenges, ancient wisdom that explains contemporary puzzles, traditional crafts that suggest new approaches to emerging technologies. But more than just historical parallels, the research process uncovered fresh ways of seeing familiar struggles that made everyday challenges suddenly visible in new light.

These weren't just clever metaphors or repackaged advice - they were practical frameworks that emerged when systematic exploration met human judgement about what helps people navigate life's challenges. The insights came from the research process itself, not from any predetermined framework I brought to the project.

What Makes This Different

This isn't comprehensive coverage of everything humans have thought - that would require multiple lifetimes and result in an encyclopaedia no one would read. Instead, it's a curated collection of insights that still matter, still work and still help people navigate the fundamental challenges of being human.

Each of the forty themes addresses one essential aspect of human experience - from reading your own emotions clearly to understanding what gives life meaning, from building relationships that last to facing mortality with wisdom. The goal isn't to tell you what to think, but to offer you clearer ways of thinking about questions you're already wrestling with.

The insights span centuries and cultures, but they speak directly to the choices you face today. How to maintain attention in a world designed to fragment it. How to build habits that serve your values. How to love deeply in an age of distraction. How to create meaningful work and authentic relationships. How to face uncertainty with wisdom rather than anxiety.

What emerged may be the first book-length synthesis of enduring human wisdom created through transparent human - AI collaboration.

Why Now

We stand at a moment of broader access to human knowledge than any previous generation has enjoyed, yet many people feel more confused than ever about what matters. We can research any topic instantly, yet struggle to distinguish between information and wisdom. We're more connected than ever through technology, yet often feel isolated in ways that human presence once solved.

Artificial Intelligence systems are now capable of handling routine cognitive tasks, generating content and even simulating aspects of human interaction. This raises profound questions about what remains essentially human and worth cultivating. At the same time, AI capabilities are advancing rapidly, with significant disagreement among researchers about how quickly transformative changes might arrive. Whether transitions unfold over years or decades, the preservation and transmission of human wisdom deserves attention now.

The answer isn't to resist these changes - they're already here. The answer is to ground ourselves more deeply in what makes life meaningful before we decide how to use our powerful new tools. To understand the thread we're carrying before we determine what to add to it or pass forward.

The Thread Continues

This book represents one attempt to identify and preserve what matters most about human experience. It's not the final word on any of these topics, but rather a distillation designed to help you think more clearly about the many choices that shape your days and years.

The thread is in your hands now. What you do with it - how you live these insights, share them with others and pass them forward - becomes part of the story that future generations will inherit.

Introduction

The Human Thread

You check your phone at 6:47 AM. Fourteen notifications wait: work emails, family messages, news alerts. Three require immediate response. Five can wait. Six are irrelevant but designed to look urgent. By 9 AM, you've fielded questions from your team, responded to a client crisis and scrolled through headlines about everyday events you can't influence. Lunch brings more messages - a friend's relationship crisis, your daughter's career concerns, a colleague asking for feedback on their proposal. By evening, you wonder if there's a clearer way to navigate all this - not drowning in information, but understanding what deserves your attention.

That question - what deserves your attention - is what this book answers. Not by adding more information to an already overwhelming flow, but by identifying what has lasting value: the parts of humanity's thread that deserve preservation and transmission. Not everything humans have thought, but what continues to help people navigate the fundamental challenges of being human.

How This Book Works

Think of this as learning to weave your own strand into humanity's ongoing thread. The book distils wisdom into six parts, each strengthening different aspects of how we flourish:

Part 1: The Self - Your foundation. Before you can navigate relationships or make good choices about work and technology, you need to understand your own inner compass. These ten themes help you read your emotions clearly, build sustainable habits, care for your energy and develop the emotional intelligence that underlies everything else. Think of this as learning to tune your most important instrument - yourself.

Part 2: Relationships & Society - How we connect. No one flourishes in isolation - we're wired for connection, shaped by community and find meaning through our bonds with others. These ten themes explore how love works, how to build friendships that last, navigate family dynamics and communicate across differences. From intimate partnerships to broader questions of justice and culture, this is about the social fabric that holds human life together.

Part 3: The World & Beyond - Your wider context. We don't live in isolation but as part of larger systems - natural, economic, technological and cultural. These themes help you understand your relationship with nature, money, technology, art and the great questions of mortality and time. This is about finding your place in the larger story of human civilisation.

Part 4: Being Human in the Age of AI - Navigating our moment. How do we maintain our essential humanity as artificial intelligence reshapes work, relationships, creativity and knowledge itself? This part applies the timeless insights from the first three parts to our current technological frontier, showing how the same principles that have guided human flourishing for centuries help us stay human in the age of machines.

Part 5: Partnership - What happens when humans guide AI rather than automate. Ten partnerships across medicine, climate, justice and beyond show what becomes possible when human wisdom steers machine capability.

Part 6: Beyond Partnership - What happens if partnership becomes impossible. What must we preserve if AI systems move beyond our ability to guide them?

Each of the themes follows the same pattern: one big insight, one memorable analogy to help you remember it and a few practical steps you can take today. These insights work together as an integrated system. The emotional intelligence you develop in Part 1 helps you navigate the relationship challenges in Part 2. The wisdom about time and change prepares you for whatever technological transitions lie ahead in Parts 4, 5 and 6.

What "Carrying the Thread" Actually Means

Understanding what you carry doesn't mean becoming a passive vessel for inherited wisdom. It means consciously engaging with insights that have helped humans flourish across centuries and cultures, testing them against your own experience and adding your discoveries to the ongoing conversation.

When you learn to read your emotions as signals rather than static, you're participating in humanity's long exploration of conscious response rather than reaction. When you build habits that serve your values, you're contributing to our collective understanding of how human change works. When you focus deeply despite digital distractions, you're preserving a capacity that may become increasingly valuable.

This is what wisdom looks like in practice: not perfect knowledge, but better navigation of the questions every generation faces. Not having all the answers, but asking questions that lead to living better. Not eliminating uncertainty, but moving through it with greater skill and less fear. Each part builds your capacity to thrive in a different domain. Together, they form a complete system for living with clarity, purpose and joy regardless of how fast the world changes around you. The goal isn't to master everything at once, but to have reliable maps for whatever territory you're crossing.

The future will bring changes we can't predict - technological, environmental, social and personal. But the fundamental questions about what makes life meaningful, how to love well, how to face uncertainty with courage and how to contribute something valuable during our brief time here remain. These questions persist across all circumstances.

Human wisdom exists because each generation has faced these challenges and discovered insights worth preserving. Now it's your turn to carry that thread forward, to add your own understanding to it and to pass on what you've learned about what really matters.

Paul Iliffe

Part 1

THE SELF

Where to Begin

This book begins with the self because self-awareness is the lens through which you read everything else. How you interpret relationships, engage with technology or approach big questions all depends partly on understanding your own patterns.

The ten themes in Part 1 aren't about optimising yourself - they're about seeing yourself clearly.

The human thread starts with you.

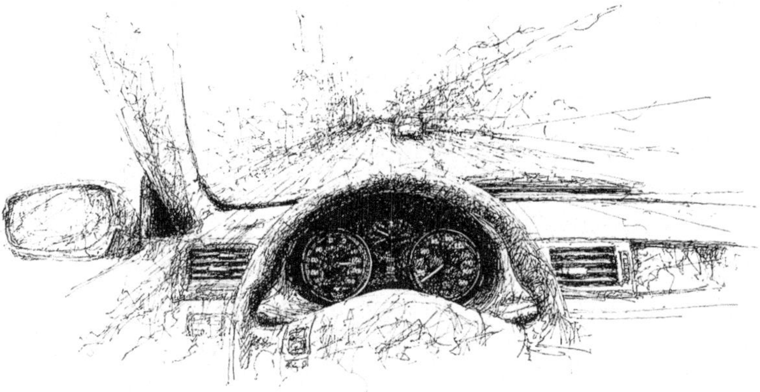

1

Identity & Self-Awareness

Understanding who you are and how you think

You arrive at the roundabout just as it starts raining. You check your speedo, then back to the merging traffic. The dashboard gauges show exactly what's happening inside your car - fuel level, speed, engine temperature. The windscreen shows what's happening outside - other drivers, road conditions and possible hazards ahead. Your mind works the same way. You have inner gauges that track your thoughts and feelings and an outward view that monitors what's actually happening around you. Better decisions come from learning to read both instruments clearly and trusting the right one at the right moment.

In ancient Athens, Socrates noticed something unsettling about human awareness. The Oracle at Delphi had proclaimed him the wisest man in Greece, which puzzled him. So he tested this by questioning politicians, poets and craftsmen - the supposed experts of his time. What he found was that they knew far less than they claimed and more importantly, they didn't realise their own ignorance. Socrates was different: he knew what he didn't know. His famous conclusion - "The unexamined life is not worth living"[1] - wasn't about achieving perfect self-knowledge. It was about learning to read your inner dashboard accurately.

People often misread their gauges. They confuse what they hope is true about themselves with what actually is.[2] But like any skilled driver, you can learn to calibrate your instruments. The Roman emperor Marcus Aurelius filled twelve books of Meditations[3] with exactly this kind of daily practice - noting his reactions, checking his assumptions, adjusting his responses. He wasn't seeking perfection but accuracy, the same quality that lets an experienced driver navigate confidently through poor weather.

Your attention works like the windscreen - it shows you what's happening outside, but it can get clouded by assumptions or distracted by irrelevant details. Experienced professionals never trust their attention alone in critical moments. They use systematic checks[4] - pilots with pre-flight checklists, surgeons with procedural protocols - to catch what memory might miss and prevent errors their confidence might cause.

This same systematic awareness develops through simple practice. Some people use this approach: before any important conversation or decision, they take thirty seconds to predict how it will go. Afterward, they compare what actually happened with what they expected and notice the gaps. This trains the same calibration skill[5] that guided ancient philosophers and modern professionals.

This insight spans centuries because it's based on how minds actually work. We can misjudge our own motivations and miss the factors influencing our choices.[6] The fix isn't to distrust all self-reflection, but to cross-check your inner readings against external evidence. If you say you value focus but your phone shows sixty notifications checked before lunch, believe the data. If you think you're a good listener but people keep repeating themselves, trust the pattern. Behaviour serves as the mirror that doesn't flatter but tells the truth.

The roundabout ahead is clearing now. You check your mirrors, signal left and merge smoothly into the flow. Dashboard and windscreen working together, each showing you what you need to know. Your inner gauges calibrated through small daily practices, your attention clear enough to see what's actually happening around you. This is self-awareness in action - not perfect knowledge of who you are, but the skill to read your instruments clearly and navigate wisely through whatever conditions you meet.

What Really Matters:
Know when to read your dashboard (your thoughts and feelings) and when to watch the windscreen (what's actually happening around you).

2

Habits & Behaviour

The patterns and choices that shape daily life

Everyone thinks consistency means perfection - one skipped day destroys a habit. Walk across any university campus and you'll see proof of the opposite. Thin brown lines cut diagonally across green lawns, threading between buildings where no official path was laid. Students skip these shortcuts for weeks during exam season when they're rushing to the library entrance instead. Grass grows back slightly. But the first person to walk the diagonal route after exams finds the track still there, still easier to follow than fighting through untrodden lawn. Town planners call them 'desire lines'[7] and your habits work exactly the same way.

Behaviour change isn't about willpower or finding the perfect system. It's about understanding that habits are well-worn paths through your day. Every time you repeat the same small action in the same context, you press a track into your routine that becomes easier to follow than to avoid. This process takes around two months for simple behaviours.[8] But the pattern holds even with gaps - missing the odd day doesn't erase your progress. The path survives gaps. You're not building perfection. You're wearing a track that endures."

This wisdom appears across centuries and cultures. The early Christian monastics understood this principle with striking clarity. These communities structured their days around precise environmental cues. The 6th-century Rule of St Benedict fixed prayer to set times throughout the day and night[9] - Lauds at dawn, Vespers at sunset, Compline before sleep. The community gathered at these appointed hours, so devotion relied on routine rather than mood.

William James, the pioneering American psychologist, recognised this same pattern in his own work while writing in the 1890s. Despite struggling with depression and scattered attention, James maintained extraordinary productivity through deliberate routine. 'Habit is thus the enormous flywheel of society,' he wrote, 'its most precious conservative agent.'[10] James understood that his literary output came not from inspiration but from the accumulated force of small, repeated actions in a consistent context.

Today's behavioural science echoes this. In one student diary study, about 40% of daily actions were habitual rather than freshly decided.[11] We are, quite literally, creatures of context and repetition. The monastery's appointed hours and James's deliberate routine both demonstrate the same principle: stable environmental cues trigger learned responses,[12] freeing mental energy for the work that matters.

Take Sonia for example who wants to read more but keeps checking her social media instead. Rather than setting ambitious reading goals, she tries something almost embarrassingly simple: every morning while making the bed, she places a book on the pillow. At bedtime, she has to physically move the book to get under the covers, which naturally leads to reading 'just one page' before sleep. Six months later, she's read more books than in the previous three years combined.

You're not trying to transform your entire life overnight. You're laying a single, clear track that your day can follow. The goal isn't perfection; it's repetition in a consistent context. When things go wrong - and they will - treat slips as bends in the path, not proof that the path doesn't exist.

The best opportunities come during fresh starts. People are more motivated after birthdays and New Year's Day.[13] Major transitions offer unique opportunities. A house move, new job or shifted schedule breaks old automatic patterns[14] and gives you a chance to draw new desire lines. This is when to establish your cues and arrange your environment - before old patterns reassert themselves. You're not fighting against established tracks - you're the first person walking across fresh grass.

What Really Matters:
Choose the route you want to walk, then walk it until walking anywhere else feels like the detour.

3

Attention & Mindfulness

Staying present and training focus

Around 335 BCE, Aristotle founded his famous Peripatetic School in Athens where he taught his students while walking through covered pathways. Peripatetic literally means "walking around." Research confirms that walking improves performance on certain creative thinking tasks compared to sitting still.[15] But Aristotle's deeper insight wasn't about walking itself - it was recognising that deliberate practices shape how well we think.

What Aristotle understood was that the quality of our thinking depends on the quality of our attention and this attention can be trained through simple, repeated practices. Walking was just one method. Monastic communities developed disciplined spiritual practices around the rhythm of daily prayers. Japanese tea masters created ceremonies that transformed preparing and drinking tea into contemplative practice. Roman Emperor Marcus Aurelius during military campaigns practised what he called "confining yourself to the present". He would write down exercises in his daily journals to return his scattered mind to the present moment.[16]

They figured out the same fundamental truth: attention is the master skill that determines every other aspect of human experience. As psychologist William James observed in 1890, "The faculty of voluntarily bringing back a wandering attention, over and over again, is the very root of judgement, character and will."[17] When you can choose where your mind focuses, you can choose how you respond to life rather than merely reacting to it.

This ancient wisdom matters more now than ever. We live in an era of engineered distraction where powerful technologies compete for our attention. Your phone buzzes. A notification appears. An algorithm suggests the next video. These aren't accidents - they're designed to grab and keep your attention.[18] These constant interruptions come at a cost: we lose practice with the sustained attention our ancestors developed naturally. Learning to direct your own attention, regardless of what's trying to steal it, is a skill humans have always needed and fortunately, it's one you can train.

Consider the simple act of drinking your morning tea. Steam curls upward as you prepare your first cup, creating a moment that millions encounter daily - a brief pause between sleeping and rushing, between private self and public face. Most of us drink mindlessly while our thoughts race ahead to the day's demands. But this moment contains something our ancestors would recognise: these three minutes offer a chance to tune your attention like a musician tunes an instrument before performing.

Elizabeth, a graphic designer in London, learned this during one of the most stressful periods of her career. Drowning in back-to-back video calls and impossible deadlines, her mornings had become a blur of checking her phone while gulping tea, her mind already racing through the day before she'd even left her kitchen. When her therapist daughter suggested something almost insultingly simple - drink your first sip of tea like it was the most important thing in the world - Elizabeth nearly dismissed it. But the next morning at 6:45, when her kettle clicked off, she tried it. She put down her phone, felt the weight of the warm mug between her palms, took one deliberate sip and tasted the bitter zest of bergamot as its warmth spread across her tongue. "It sounds ridiculous," she says six months later, "but those moments became the most reliable part of my day. Everything that followed felt more deliberate, less reactive."

Mindfulness practice trains two core abilities: focused attention - returning your mind to a chosen anchor like the warmth of your mug - and open monitoring - noticing whatever thoughts, sensations or emotions arise without getting swept away by them.[19] Both strengthen what psychologists call meta-awareness: your ability to observe your own mental processes. When you notice your mind has wandered to tomorrow's presentation during your morning tea, you're developing the same skill that lets you pause before responding angrily to a difficult email.

Beyond awareness itself, this mindfulness practice can reduce anxiety and depression while improving emotion regulation and attention.[20] Yet researchers do caution that mindfulness isn't a remedy for all situations - effects may vary considerably across individuals and contexts.[21] The real transformation lies in something harder to measure: the difference between living on autopilot and living with conscious choice in each moment. Ancient traditions called it different names - Buddhist mindfulness, Christian contemplation, Stoic prosoche - but they all recognised attention as the gateway to wisdom.

Tomorrow morning, when your kettle turns off and steam rises from your cup, you might try something. The phone can wait. That first sip, taken as if you'd never tasted tea before, offers a chance to observe what your mind does with one moment of pure attention.[22] This is where attention training can begin - not in a monastery or meditation retreat, but in choosing to notice what's happening right now.

What Really Matters:
Where you direct your attention shapes everything else - your capacity for clear thinking, conscious choice and presence.

4

Emotional Intelligence & Self-Compassion

Understanding feelings and treating yourself kindly

Your emotions aren't the problem - the story you tell yourself about them is. Back in first-century Rome, a Stoic philosopher named Epictetus stumbled onto something that would change how we think about emotions forever. Born a slave, he learned through brutal experience that you can't control what happens to you. But you can absolutely control how you interpret it. He discovered a principle often paraphrased as "It's not the things themselves that upset us, but what we tell ourselves about those things."[23] Epictetus identified the difference between information and interpretation - between the signal your emotions send and the stories your mind adds.

Think of emotions as a radio broadcasting useful information about what matters and what needs your attention.[24] When your chest tightens during a difficult conversation, that's a signal that something important is happening. But then your mind starts adding static: catastrophic predictions, harsh self-judgements, stories about how everything's falling apart.

This distinction between signal and static matters. People who can distinguish their emotions precisely - irritated versus furious, worried versus panicked - tend to navigate challenges more effectively and recover from setbacks more quickly.[25] They make smarter choices instead of just reacting. You're not trying to eliminate difficult feelings or stay positive all the time. You're developing clearer reception of what your emotions are actually telling you. Then responding with both intelligence and kindness.

An ancient Buddhist text called the Sallatha Sutta describes being struck by two arrows. The first arrow is the unavoidable pain - the job rejection, the harsh criticism, the relationship ending. You didn't choose it and you can't prevent it. The second arrow is what we do to ourselves afterward: the catastrophic interpretations, the harsh self-judgement, the stories about what this means about our worth.[26] The Buddha's insight wasn't that you can avoid the first arrow. It was recognising that the second arrow - the mental anguish we pile on top - is optional. The original hurt is the signal. The stories we tell ourselves are the static.

Neuroscience offers evidence for what these traditions under-stood intuitively. When emotions spike, two quick readings can help: pleasant or unpleasant? How intense? Then comes the most important step: labelling what you're experiencing as precisely as possible. "I'm irritated and under pressure" gives you better information than "I'm stressed." This labelling technique can work by engaging your brain's naming systems while calming its alarm centres,[27] though effectiveness varies depending on context and individual differences.

Luke discovered this when a music label rejection hit harder than expected. His immediate reaction was "I'm a failure - I'll never get signed." It was pure static. But when he separated the signal from the noise, clearer information emerged. Yes, he felt gutted about losing this specific opportunity. But buried in the feedback was genuine guidance - they wanted more polished production on the tracks he'd submitted. The signal pointed towards concrete action: book studio time to remix the EP with better mixing and mastering. The static was telling him his music career was finished. Four weeks later, with stronger demos and renewed confidence, he had meetings lined up with three independent labels.

Trying to suppress difficult emotions typically backfires.[28] The feelings you push away tend to return with greater force. Emotional static isn't eliminated through suppression. It gets clarified through understanding.

Self-compassion research reveals another pattern worth noting: people who treat themselves with kindness during struggles tend to show better outcomes than those who don't.[29] This isn't about lowering standards. It's recognising that when you make a mistake, the signal might be 'I need to learn from this.' The static sounds like 'I'm worthless.' One response leads somewhere useful. The other just amplifies suffering.

What Really Matters:
Emotions are signals, not commands. Learn to distinguish the useful information from the mental static, then respond with both intelligence and kindness.

5

Health, Rest & Play

Caring for body and spirit through balance

Your wellness routine works brilliantly - until it doesn't. Elaborate systems optimised for stable conditions fail exactly when you need them most. The real question isn't 'how do I optimise my health?' It's 'what's my backup system when everything collapses?'

She was reading her redundancy letter when everything shifted. It was precisely 2:47 pm on a Tuesday afternoon. One of those moments that splits your life into before and after. Single mum, mortgage hanging over her head and zero savings to cushion the blow. Her elaborate wellness routine? Gone overnight. Those 6 AM gym sessions, the Sunday meal prep marathons, even her meditation apps suddenly felt like expensive luxuries she couldn't justify. You'd expect her health to nosedive. Instead, she stumbled onto something our ancestors figured out centuries ago: the art of intelligent minimums.

Within a week, she'd unconsciously created what she started calling her "minimum viable self." Six hours of sleep - same window every night. Daily walk while her daughter was at school. One proper meal they'd share together. Some days she managed more. Other days, this baseline kept her going. When work opportunities eventually turned up, rebuilding felt possible because she'd never actually hit rock bottom. As stability returned, so did her sleep - gradually back to seven and a half hours.

When your phone's battery drops to 5%, everything non-essential starts to shut down. Screen dims. Apps close quietly in the background. What's left? Just enough juice to keep the core system ticking until you find a charger. She'd built herself the same backup system without realising it.

This goes completely against wellness advice that assumes you've got endless time, energy and motivation. Those perfect morning routines and comprehensive fitness programmes that look great on TV? Real life laughs at them. Sick kids, impossible deadlines, family drama - they'll steamroll elaborate plans every time. Then comes the all-or-nothing thinking that convinces you you've failed. Actually, you've just been using the wrong blueprint.

The Jewish Sabbath is perhaps humanity's oldest surviving designed rest system. From Friday sunset to Saturday nightfall, an entire day withdraws from productive activity. No work, no commerce, no striving. What's remarkable isn't the rest itself but the structure protecting it. The Sabbath doesn't depend on feeling rested enough to stop. It arrives every seven days whether you're ready or not, whether your work is finished or not. The ancient rabbis understood that if rest waits until all your work is complete, rest never comes. Life always has one more urgent task. So they created an unmovable boundary - one day in seven, protected regardless of circumstances.

This wisdom connects to how human biology actually operates. Sleep anchors everything else because it's controlled by your body's internal clock.[30] Most healthy adults function best after seven to nine hours, though individual differences matter hugely.[31] When life squeezes available sleep time, consistency helps - but restoring at least seven hours should remain the priority. During temporary rough patches, maintaining the same sleep window supports your circadian rhythm while you work to restore adequate duration. Your internal clock takes its main cues from light - morning brightness and dimmed evening screens can help maintain rhythm during rough patches.[32]

Movement comes second in the non-negotiable list. The World Health Organisation frames it perfectly: "any movement is better than none."[33] It could be as simple as ten-minute walks or bodyweight squats while your kettle boils. The goal isn't fitness achievement - it's maintaining that crucial connection between mind and body that sedentary life slowly erodes.

Technology either props up or sabotages your backup system. Phone notifications affect attention in lab studies, though real-world impact varies massively by context.[34] During overwhelming periods, "do not disturb" modes create protected restoration windows. Simple screen dimming after sunset might help preserve sleep quality for some people. Setting devices to quiet by default, then deliberately adding back only what earns its place - most people find that predictable low-stimulation periods help them unwind.

Your minimum viable self isn't permanent - it's a platform for rebuilding. During crisis mode, you protect sleep windows while everything else flexes. When capacity returns, you layer back the rest. But you never start from absolute zero again.

What Really Matters:
Build your minimum viable self before you need it - it's not a limitation, it's the foundation that ensures you never hit absolute zero.

6

Meaning & Happiness

What gives life meaning and how joy can emerge

Most happiness advice sounds the same. Find your bliss. Follow your dreams. Focus on yourself first. We treat joy like a flame that needs protecting - cupping our hands around it, shielding it from others who might somehow steal our light. But happiness works more like an actual flame than we realise. The counterintuitive truth about fire changes what we think we know about finding meaning.

Here's how flames actually work. When you light another candle from your own, your flame doesn't get smaller. This isn't splitting a pie or dividing resources - it's creating more light in the world while keeping exactly what you started with. Picture two candles in a darkened room. When the first lights the second, both flames illuminate more space than either could alone. The combined flames don't compete; they amplify each other's reach.

This insight reaches back through centuries, though not quite how you might expect. The Olympic torch relay, created as a propaganda spectacle for the 1936 Berlin Games[35], was later repurposed to celebrate a shared, purposeful journey - capturing what the ancient Greeks understood about sacred fire: that a flame gains meaning not from being hoarded but from being shared. It connects individual efforts into a luminous chain that spans continents and generations.

Each runner receives the flame, carries it forward, then passes it on. No runner loses anything in the transfer - they become part of something larger while the flame burns as bright as ever.

The torch also carries meaning across generations. Each runner doesn't just feel good in the moment; they become part of a story that stretches from ancient Olympia to future games they'll never see. This is what psychologists call the difference between hedonic and eudaimonic wellbeing[36] - feeling good versus living meaningfully. When you light another's candle, you're not just boosting mood; you're connecting yourself to something larger than your individual existence.

Research in multiple countries finds that when people spend small amounts on others, they often feel happier than when they spend the same on themselves - though this varies across different cultures and personalities[37]. Acts of kindness, performed regularly, are linked with small but reliable average improvements in wellbeing for the person doing them[38].

When you help others, several things happen simultaneously. You stop constantly monitoring your own mood and energy levels, which alone reduces psychological strain. Many acts of service also create clear goals with immediate feedback - conditions that psychologist Mihaly Csikszentmihalyi found make flow more likely[39]. Flow is that state of deep absorption where you lose track of time because you're fully engaged in what you're doing. As he found out, "the best moments usually occur when a person's body or mind is stretched to its limits"[40] in service of something meaningful. This stretching often happens when we're in service to others - solving a problem for a neighbour, creating something with a team - which creates the very state of flow that becomes a pathway to deep satisfaction. Instead of resenting what you lack, you feel grateful for what you can offer.

This approach sidesteps common traps that sabotage well-intentioned efforts at happiness. It's not toxic positivity, which insists you should always feel upbeat and ignores the fact that difficult emotions carry essential information[41]. It's not perfectionism: small, consistent acts of lighting others' candles matter more than grand gestures that leave you depleted. And it's not social comparison - your contribution creates value regardless of anyone else's volunteer hours posted on social media. The principle works best when you have some emotional reserves to draw from. If you're already overwhelmed with caregiving responsibilities or dealing with your own major challenges, stabilising your situation before focusing outward makes sense.

The flame metaphor reveals why the self-focus approach fails so consistently. When you cup your hands around your own candle, protecting it from the world, you create the very isolation that snuffs it out. Flames need air to breathe, space to grow and purpose beyond mere survival. They thrive when they're used to illuminate the darkness for others to navigate by.

Rather than endlessly asking "what can I get?", consider what light you might share. The answer isn't about collecting brightness for yourself, but about becoming part of the light that guides others through darkness - connecting your brief flame to something that burns long after you're gone.

What Really Matters:
Your flame of happiness grows brighter when you light another's candle.

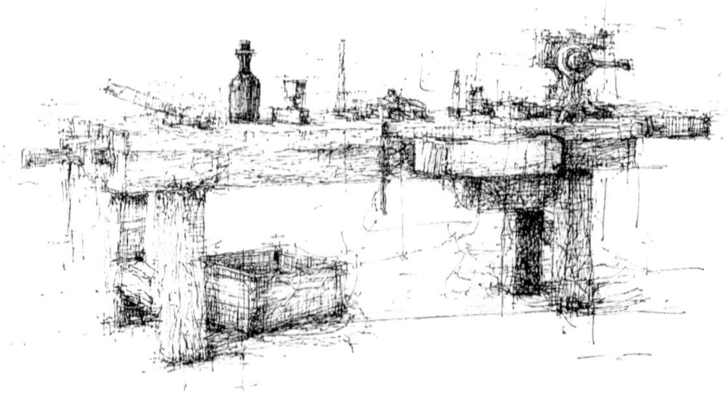

7

Learning & Growth Mindset

How we develop and expand our abilities

When your time is short and stakes are high, sloppy learning can cost you twice. Like a carpenter who skips measuring, learners who cram without strategy build skills that wobble under pressure. The remedy isn't more hours at the bench - it's better technique. Your mind works like a well-oiled workshop where skill grows by making useful pieces with the right tools, not by rushing through projects.

In 1885, German psychologist Hermann Ebbinghaus made a startling discovery that every craftsman would recognise. Using himself as his only subject, he spent months memorising lists of meaningless syllables, then testing how much he could recall after different intervals. What he mapped was exactly how quickly the human mind forgets. Forgetting drops steeply within hours and continues across the first day, then slows[42]. It turns out reviewing material at spaced intervals improves long-term retention; the optimal gap depends on how long you need to remember[43]. What seemed like a flaw in human memory was actually the mind showing us its preferred working rhythm.

Think of learning as craftsmanship. Skilled builders focus on three fundamental techniques that separate lasting work from quick fixes. They test their memory of procedures before checking instructions - retrieving knowledge from experience rather than simply rereading[44]. They space their work over days and weeks instead of cramming everything into marathon sessions. And they mix related skills in the same session, learning not just how each tool works but when to use it, though the benefit varies by task. [45] It's not theory - it's how skill actually builds when precision matters.

Sonia experienced this during her first attempt at learning British Sign Language. As an occupational therapist working with deaf clients through interpreters, she'd always felt something was lost in translation. So she enrolled in evening classes. For two weeks, she followed her usual pattern: filming signs on her phone, scrolling through videos before bed, feeling productive. But when asked to sign "How are you feeling today?" without notes, her hands fumbled. She couldn't remember basic movements she'd watched dozens of times.

Week three, her instructor changed the rules. "Phones away. All of them." Sonia panicked - how would she remember without recording? But that evening, she tried something different. Phone in drawer, she started signing to herself from memory - alphabet, greetings, that day's conversation. Her hands kept stopping. She'd mark what she'd forgotten, then test herself again the next session before checking anything.

Within three weeks, signs appeared without conscious thought. By week eight, she managed an entire appointment in BSL with a deaf client. The woman's face when she realised they could communicate directly made every frustrating evening worthwhile.[46]

What made the difference wasn't more hours of study. It was working with her mind's actual rhythm instead of against it. Testing herself before checking notes showed her exactly what she didn't know. Spacing the practice over weeks let each session build on properly consolidated memory rather than cramming everything together. Signing to her empty room forced her to retrieve the movements from memory rather than passively watching someone else demonstrate them. The spacing and retrieval had done their work.

Like any craftsman, learners need proper support without mistaking it for the main work. Sleep consolidates what you've built - during rest, the brain replays and strengthens the connections you made through retrieval and spacing.[47] Brief movement helps maintain focus.[48] But these are supports, not shortcuts - no amount of rest substitutes for deliberate practice with feedback. The craftsman's workshop teaches us that skill builds through patient attention to technique, not frantic activity. Each practice session becomes another careful cut, another joint that will hold under pressure.

What really matters
Work with your mind's patterns, not against them.

8

Recognition

Seeing invisible support systems

You're standing at the edge of a quiet beach. The tide has just gone out. From a distance, the landscape looks empty - grey sand, flat stones, a few pools of water left behind. You're about to move on. But something catches your eye. You crouch down beside a shallow rock pool. Inside, a miniature world: darting fish no longer than a paperclip, tiny crabs weaving through strands of seaweed, anemones anchored to stones.

None of this was visible until you looked closely. From above, it seemed like nothing was there. But these rock pools held life the whole time - just hidden from the angle you were using.

Most of us live this way. We focus on the ocean - the big moments, the obvious wins, the visible effort. But what often sustains those moments is what we don't see: the ecosystem of quiet support just beneath our attention.

The colleague who quietly covered your mistakes during that crucial month. The teacher who spotted something in your work before you saw it yourself. The partner who reorganised their schedule so you could meet a deadline. The friend who sent the article that shifted your thinking at exactly the right moment.

These contributions don't announce themselves. They work like rock pools - vital, intricate, easy to walk past if you're still watching the horizon. When people practise noticing benefits and who provided them, something shifts.[49] They start seeing connections and support they'd been missing. Most of us rely on networks of support that are easy to overlook.[50]

The Roman philosopher Seneca understood this pattern. In his work De Beneficiis (On Benefits), he described gratitude as a three-part cycle: giving, receiving and returning. He argued that properly recognising a benefit - truly seeing what someone has done for you - creates an impulse to reciprocate. The social bond strengthens not just through the original help but through the conscious recognition of it.[51] This wasn't just abstract theory - Seneca was describing how social relationships functioned in Roman life and it still applies today. Whether it's a favour between friends or support at work, relationships tend to last when contributions are acknowledged.

Your morning tea required growers who tended plants for months, blenders who refined the leaves, shippers who coordinated logistics across continents and retailers who stocked and sold it to you. Each role was essential but most remain invisible. The success gets attributed to whoever presented the final result. The rock pools that made it possible stay submerged.

Workplace studies by psychologists Adam Grant and Francesca Gino found that when managers briefly thanked employees for their help, those employees became more willing to assist others - not just the manager who thanked them.[52] The recognition strengthened the helping patterns themselves. It works by making visible the support that was already there but easy to miss.

Some situations genuinely lack adequate support and seeing that clearly matters too. The goal isn't universal appreciation but accurate perception of what's actually there. When you understand the infrastructure available to support you, you become both more humble and more confident. Humble because you see how much you depend on others. Confident because you understand the actual support systems around you.

What Really Matters:
The most vital support systems often hide in plain sight while you're watching the horizon.

9

Resilience

Recovering from setbacks with flexible strength

Watch a bamboo grove in a typhoon and you'll see what real resilience looks like - not rigid resistance, but intelligent flexibility that survives the storm intact. Each stalk bends deeply with the wind, sometimes touching the ground, then springs back upright when the pressure passes. This isn't weakness. It's a sophisticated survival strategy refined over millions of years.

In first-century Rome, the Stoic philosopher Epictetus discovered this principle the hard way. Born into slavery, he learned that trying to control the uncontrollable leads to misery. Real freedom came from bending consciously with what you cannot change whilst preserving energy for what actually matters. "Some things are within our power," he wrote, "whilst others are not."[53] Epictetus and his fellow Stoic philosophers mapped when to bend and when to hold firm.[54]

What makes bamboo particularly instructive is how individual stalks survive better in groves than in isolation. Their root systems interlock underground, creating a network where each plant supports the others. When wind pressure threatens to topple one stalk, the connected roots of neighbouring plants provide stability. The grove bends together, shares the load and returns upright as a collective system. Resilience isn't just about individual flexibility - it's built into the structure of mutual support.

Research on human resilience shows a parallel pattern. People with stronger social relationships live longer - about 50% lower mortality risk in meta-analytic studies.[55] Like bamboo groves with interlocking roots, humans survive pressure better when they're connected to support systems. The strength isn't just in the individual - it's in the network.

James learned this the hard way. When his agency's largest pitch deadline moved up by ten days, he attempted the rigid oak approach. He worked through weekends, skipped meals, refused help from his team saying "I've got this." He insisted on handling every detail himself - the strategy deck, the financial projections, the client presentation. Two sleepless nights of solo grinding left him exhausted. He delivered a polished but rushed pitch that fell flat. Like a rigid tree in high wind, he broke under pressure he thought he was strong enough to resist.

Months later, similar pressure hit - a major client demanding delivery three weeks early. Instead of breaking under isolated pressure, he bent like bamboo in a grove. He called his business partner: could he take over client communications for the next fortnight whilst James focused purely on production? He asked his wife: could they postpone the planned weekend away by a month? He contacted two freelancers he'd worked with before: could they handle the final quality checks?

Each request required swallowing pride and admitting he couldn't do it alone. But like bamboo stalks with interlocking roots, the support network held firm when pressure hit. Three weeks later, the delivery went out on the new timeline. James had bent - simplified some specifications, delegated responsibilities, acknowledged his limitations. But nothing essential broke. The client relationship strengthened. His business partner felt more valued. His wife appreciated being asked rather than ignored. The freelancers got paid work and stronger connections for future projects. The grove survived the storm together.

What Really Matters:
Like bamboo in a typhoon, true resilience isn't about never bending - it's about yielding consciously with support from others so you don't break what matters most.

10

Creativity

Expressing ideas and making something new

Luke's first commission at the production studio came with a tight deadline. The client wanted a film score theme by Friday. His colleague Jack, also a veteran composer, who'd been there for years, had a clear strategy: work in isolation all week, then deliver the polished final version. Jack believed that showing rough work invited interference and diluted your vision. Better to perfect things privately, then present them fully formed.

Luke tried that same approach on Monday and Tuesday. By Wednesday morning, he had something technically competent that felt hollow. He couldn't figure out why. The chord progressions worked. The production was clean. But something essential was missing and he'd run out of perspective staring at the same screen for three days.

So Luke did what felt risky: he started sharing his work-in-progress with a few colleagues. Not a polished showpiece - actual rough drafts with obvious gaps and tentative choices. One colleague pointed out that his build felt predictable. Another suggested the emotional tone didn't match the film's themes. A third heard something in a transitional section that Luke had almost cut. Each conversation shifted his direction slightly. By Thursday evening, the track had evolved through multiple iterations - some elements abandoned entirely, others emerging from fragments he'd barely noticed.

Jack delivered a polished track on Friday. It was competent. It sounded like his previous work. The client accepted it without enthusiasm. Luke delivered a track that had been shaped by ongoing dialogue throughout the week. The client said it captured something they hadn't known they were looking for and it became the film's main theme.

This isn't a story about productivity or perfectionism. It's about the fundamental misunderstanding that kills more creative work than any lack of talent: the belief that creative vision develops through private perfection rather than shared imperfection.[56]

The Japanese Zen teacher Shunryu Suzuki captured something essential about this process when he observed that 'in the beginner's mind there are many possibilities, but in the expert's there are few.'[57] This isn't just philosophical wisdom - it describes the psychological trap that catches creators like Jack and Luke. Jack's expert mind sought certainty and completion, closing itself off to possibility. Each hour of private polishing narrowed his options until his track became a polished version of his usual approach. Luke's willingness to share rough work kept his beginner's mind active - open to surprise, to learning, to the unexpected directions that emerge when you expose work before it feels ready. The beginner's mind isn't about lacking skill. It's about maintaining the openness that allows skill to develop in new directions.

Creative work functions like learning to dance - not performing a flawless solo, but practicing with others through generous awkwardness. Jack's expert mind sought the perfect performance before anyone watched. Luke's beginner's mind stayed open to stumbling in view of others, discovering his rhythm through the process itself. The willingness to dance badly in company is what teaches you to dance well.

We see this across other creative disciplines too. Visual artists share unfinished canvases with fellow painters, not seeking approval but using external eyes to spot what they've stopped seeing themselves. Writers show rough drafts to trusted readers. Filmmakers screen early cuts to small audiences. What changes through these exchanges isn't just the work itself - it's the creator's ability to recognise which elements serve their vision and which don't.

Eric Tucker understood the risk of never joining that conversation. A working-class painter from Warrington, he spent sixty years painting scenes of industrial life in his front room, producing over 400 masterful works but sharing almost none. When his family opened his house as a gallery after his death in 2018, 1,500 people queued around the block.[58] His authentic voice had been there all along - but he'd never let it join the conversation that could have shaped both his work and his world.

Tucker's technical mastery was undeniable. But creativity isn't just about making good things in private. It's about letting your work exist in dialogue with others - not to seek approval, but to discover what your work might become through that exchange. Tucker's paintings gained their power from his genuine observation of working life. But imagine what might have emerged if he'd shared them as he developed his work. If peoples reactions had helped him refine which scenes captured something essential and which were practice pieces.

What Really Matters:
Creativity isn't about having perfect ideas - it's about having the courage to dance badly in public until you discover your own rhythm.

Part 2

RELATIONSHIPS & SOCIETY

Beyond Yourself

Now the lens widens. Humans are fundamentally social creatures. We think, feel and find meaning through our connections with others - family, friends, colleagues, communities, the wider society we help create and that shapes us in return.

The ten themes in Part 2 explore how we actually connect in a world full of competing demands on our attention. How love works when life gets complicated. How to maintain friendships across busy adult schedules. How to navigate conflict without damaging what matters. How to build communities that welcome difference while maintaining shared purpose.

None of this happens in isolation. The clearer you see yourself, the better you can see others.

11

Love

Forms, expressions and the science of deep connection

Elizabeth sits across from James at dinner, nodding as he explains something about a client project. Her mind drifts to tomorrow's presentation deadlines. Her phone sits face-up on the table between them, screen dark but still pulling at her attention like a phantom limb.[1] He notices her distraction, she notices him noticing, but they both pretend nothing happened. This happens most nights now and neither knows why intimacy feels so hard to find when they spend hours together in the same space.

Elizabeth has stopped stargazing without noticing. James has become like a familiar constellation to her - the pattern of his moods, his stories, his way of moving through the world. Early in their relationship, every look she gave him revealed new details. But over time, familiarity blurred the details. It is easy to glance at someone we know well and assume we already know what we'll see, forgetting that constellations shift constantly with season, weather and perspective.

Love begins to fade not when the stars burn out, but when we stop paying attention to what's actually there tonight.

Research on what psychologists call "responsive partnering" shows that relationships thrive when partners stay curious about each other's evolving inner worlds.[2] John Gottman, a psychologist who has studied thousands of couples over decades, found that lasting relationships depend less on compatibility than on noticing and responding to small "bids for connection" throughout each day.[3] Harry Reis and Phillip Shaver, researchers who pioneered our understanding of adult intimacy, discovered that closeness grows not from grand gestures but from everyday responsiveness: paying attention, answering gently, seeing what's new rather than assuming what's known.[4]

James has been sending signals - small shifts in how he talks about his work, new tensions around meaning and legacy, different ways of approaching their shared decisions. But Elizabeth has been consulting an old star chart. She responds to the person she expects him to be, rather than noticing who he is becoming. Distance grows not from betrayal or neglect, but from the subtle drift of attention.

The shift happened one evening when Elizabeth left her phone in another room during dinner. With nothing pulling her attention away, she began noticing what was actually there: the long pause James took before answering difficult questions, the way his voice changed when something truly mattered to him, the difference between his exhaustion that needed space and exhaustion that needed connection.

Our minds naturally take shortcuts with familiar things. It helps us navigate daily life, but it works against the fresh attention love requires. Partners are not fixed constellations but shifting skies. What delighted them last month may bore them now. The comfort that once reassured them might no longer fit their current struggles.

The couples who sustain connection over decades seem to understand something fundamental: love is not about finding someone whose constellation never changes, but about remaining curious about the person beside you.[5] The person you love is not always the same person they were yesterday.

What Really Matters:
Love lives in fresh seeing - the ongoing choice to look with curiosity rather than assumption, noticing who your partner is becoming rather than responding to who they used to be.

12

Friendship

Building and maintaining meaningful bonds

Adult friendships fade not from neglect but from lack of regular encounter spaces. Without the built-in rhythms of school or early career, relationships need what sociologist Ray Oldenburg called "third places" - regular gathering spots beyond home and work.[6]

In the late 1980s, Oldenburg studied how friendships survive in modern life. He noticed that strong communities shared something specific: predictable, low-pressure spaces where the same people encountered each other on a reliable rhythm. The corner cafe where locals meet for morning coffee. The park where dog owners cross paths each evening. The pub quiz team that gathers every Tuesday. These weren't grand social events requiring coordination. They were accessible spots where showing up meant you'd see familiar faces.

What made these places work wasn't the location itself. It was the pattern they created. When you know you'll see someone at the Saturday farmers market or Thursday evening yoga, friendship doesn't require elaborate planning. The rhythm does the work. Regular, informal contact in neutral spaces maintains bonds that formal dinner parties can't sustain. The relationships that endure often run on these small, repeated encounters rather than intensive catch-up sessions.

Oldenburg found that these gathering places shared common features: they were accessible without much planning, welcomed regulars and newcomers equally, conversation mattered more than consumption and the atmosphere stayed relaxed rather than status-conscious. Modern life has thinned these spaces - longer commutes, online shopping, streaming entertainment at home. But the principle still holds: friendship needs places and rhythms that make regular contact feel natural rather than effortful.

Sonia felt this gap in her own life after moving for work. Between irregular shifts and family commitments, she'd watch friendships fade despite good intentions. Coordinating dinner with old friends felt overwhelming. By the time they managed to meet, months had passed and reconnecting meant compressing everything into an awkward catch-up session - recycling old stories, apologising for the gap, promising to meet sooner next time. She needed something simpler. What if instead of elaborate plans, she just found places where she showed up regularly?

She started with Sunday morning at her local gym, same time each week. After a month, she recognised faces. After two months, brief conversations started. She added Tuesday evening yoga, then Friday morning coffee at the same cafe. Not friendship events - just predictable rhythms where familiar faces gathered.

Three months in, she discovered a former flatmate attended the same yoga class. The friendship she'd thought had faded strengthened again through these small, regular encounters. No coordination required, no pressure to catch up on months of news in one evening. Just consistent presence in the same spaces.

Communication researcher Jeffrey Hall studied friendship formation at the University of Kansas. His research with college students and recent movers found that casual friendships typically formed around 50-100 hours of contact.[7] Closer bonds required substantially more time - often 200 hours or beyond. These findings reflect specific populations, so the precise timeline may not apply universally. The broader pattern holds across contexts: friendship deepens through steady, spaced contact rather than intensive bursts.[9-11]

Regular contact often prevents many problems, but when conflicts do arise, the same principle of timely attention applies. Research on conflict repair identifies several elements people consider important in apologies: acknowledging harm, taking responsibility and offering specific ways to address it.[8] Like regular contact, repair works best when it happens quickly rather than letting tensions harden. Both recognise that relationships need deliberate care instead of assuming good intentions alone sustain connection.

Adult friendship requires this kind of attention because built-in encounter systems disappear after childhood. Without school corridors and shared daily routines, relationships must survive competing commitments and natural drift. The pattern is predictable: busy periods create temporary distance, which becomes awkwardness, which becomes permanent separation - unless connection continues through regular contact and problems get addressed while they're still manageable.

What Really Matters:
Friendship needs regular encounter spaces - find your third places and show up consistently.

13

Family

Dynamics, traditions and navigating close relationships

Elizabeth's kitchen fills with the familiar storm. Her mother texts about Sunday lunch traditions while her daughter retreats upstairs, muttering about "forced family time." Her husband fields calls from his confused elderly mother who refuses help with her smartphone but keeps missing appointments. Three generations pulling in different directions and Elizabeth feels like she's being torn apart in the middle.

Elizabeth is standing on one of humanity's oldest engineering marvels. A suspension bridge spanning time itself. Your family isn't meant to be a quiet house on a hill. It's a vast bridge flexing and humming with energy, carrying the weight of human connection across generations. One end is anchored deep in what came before. The middle deck is where you live today. The far end disappears into the fog of what will come after you.

Ancient builders understood this perfectly. Chinese engineers created suspension spans that danced with wind and weather but never broke. They understood that tension isn't the enemy of stability - it's the mechanism that makes crossing possible. The cables stretching between towers carry enormous weight precisely because they're under constant strain. Remove the tension and the bridge collapses.

Your family operates on identical engineering principles. Those cables stretching from the ancestral pillar carry things you never chose: stories, habits, recipes, faith, fears, jokes that outlived their tellers. Your grandmother's conviction that love means feeding people. Your father's way of showing care through practical help, not words. The family pattern of avoiding difficult conversations. These inherited patterns create one kind of tension.

But modern families have multiple cable systems creating their own tension patterns. There's the bridge between siblings with different values. The span connecting in-laws from different cultures. The cables carrying step-children between households. Each relationship adds complexity to the overall structure. And now digital tools have become part of the bridge itself - photo streams, shared calendars, WhatsApp groups that keep family members connected to daily life across distance.[12] These aren't separate from family dynamics; they're new materials woven into the bridge's fabric.

Structural tension serves a purpose, but harmful patterns damage the bridge itself. When her mother defends Sunday lunch traditions, she's protecting the cable that carries family connection across time. When her daughter tests the boundaries, she's checking whether the bridge can flex for her generation. This is healthy tension - the groan and hum of structure doing its work, the same dynamic flexibility that allows suspension bridges to carry weight while adapting to changing conditions.

But not all tension is structural. Where there's ongoing contempt, coercion or control - patterns that research associates with relationship deterioration[13] - it's no longer about the bridge flexing. It's a structural issue requiring repair or, in some cases, distance. The distinction matters: healthy tension connects across difference, while harmful tension patterns erode the foundation itself.

Research tracking how families spend time shows the invisible load this bridge management requires. In England and Wales, around five million people provide unpaid care,[14] much of it the infrastructure that holds intergenerational connections together. Researchers use the term "connected presence"[15] for this kind of contact - the shared photo that says "thinking of you" without demanding a response, the family calendar that keeps everyone informed without requiring a meeting. Connection without obligation.

Household divisions reveal another surprising aspect of bridge maintenance. What feels fair matters more than what measures equally.[16] One couple splits chores 50/50 and resents it. Another does 70/30 and both feel satisfied. The difference? Whether the division respects what each person values and can sustainably manage. The question isn't "are we doing this exactly equally?" but "does this feel sustainable and respectful to everyone involved?" Strong families hold inheritance and future legacy in dynamic tension through daily life. They understand the bridge's purpose is transfer, not stillness.

What Really Matters:
Family bridges need healthy tension to carry weight across generations - but harmful tension requires repair or distance.

14

Communication, Empathy & Boundaries

Connection in digital and physical spaces

You're in a heated conversation. Family tensions rising, workplace conflict brewing, that relationship discussion you've been avoiding for weeks. Instead of pausing, you push deeper into the argument. The result? Someone storms out. Relationships rupture. Trust gets damaged.

Ancient divers faced the same problem - just underwater. Harvesting sponges from the Mediterranean seabed over two millennia ago, they learned something crucial about working under pressure. The deeper you descend, the more dangerous pressure becomes if you rush. Your body cannot handle rapid pressure changes. One careless moment - dropping down too fast - and what should be exploration turns into emergency. They developed a survival principle: acknowledge the pressure, work with it gradually, never force your way through resistance.[17]

When you descend underwater, you feel it quickly - that squeeze building in your ears as water pressure increases but the air pressure in your ear canals hasn't caught up yet. You stop, pinch your nose and gently blow - balancing the pressure inside your ears with the water pressure outside. This technique, called equalisation, isn't optional.[18] Forcing a descent without managing pressure leads to ruptured eardrums, disorienting vertigo or severe inner-ear barotrauma. Every diver learns to equalise early and often.

Human conversation works exactly the same way. Emotional pressure builds, but instead of pausing to equalise, we just keep pushing deeper. The technique that saves divers applies directly to difficult conversations - acknowledge the pressure, work with it gradually, check conditions before proceeding.

Around the 5th century BCE, Buddhist teachers developed what they called "right speech" - a practice of pausing before speaking in charged moments.[19] The approach involved considering whether words would be true, helpful and timely. This worked like pressure equalisation: creating space to assess conditions before going deeper. The practice wasn't about avoiding difficult conversations but about checking your emotional pressure gauges before descending, so the conversation could reach somewhere valuable instead of causing damage. As the Dhammapada - a collection of Buddhist teachings - observes, "Better than a thousand hollow words is one word that brings peace" - the difference often comes down to managing pressure first.

Watch what happens when you hit unexpected conditions underwater. The current strengthens, stirring up sediment that clouds your vision. Your instinct says push through, but your training says otherwise. Pressure check - still manageable. Air supply - still good. You move to calmer water, wait for the murkiness to settle, then continue from a more stable position. This isn't retreat - it's intelligent pressure management.

The same pattern works in difficult conversations. You're in a team meeting when a colleague consistently interrupts others and dismisses their ideas. You feel the pressure building - chest tightening, breathing becoming shallow, that familiar heat rising in your face. That's your emotional pressure gauge signalling danger. Instead of diving straight into confrontation mode, you pause and check your gauges. Can you handle this depth right now? Are conditions right for this conversation?

After the meeting, you approach them privately: "I've noticed some tension in our discussions. Can we talk about how we collaborate?" You've just equalised the pressure. Their defensiveness softens. "I didn't realise I was doing that. I suppose I get anxious when deadlines are tight." The conversation that follows happens at a depth you can both handle, because you managed the pressure first.

Digital communication completely ignores these hard-won pressure principles. We fire off texts when we're emotionally flooded - like attempting a dive with faulty pressure gauges. We try to handle complex emotional topics over email where tone gets lost - like diving in murky water with no visibility. We schedule difficult video calls when we're already exhausted - like diving when your air supply is already low.

The pressure equalisation principle reveals why this fails so consistently. Text messages strip out vocal tone and facial expressions that help us gauge emotional pressure in real time.[20] Email threads about sensitive topics build pressure with each exchange, but nobody can tell when someone's about to hit their limit.[21] Video calls seem intimate but can increase pressure through constant self-monitoring and screen fatigue.[22]

Some conversations need the full pressure-sensing equipment of face-to-face contact. Others work better with the controlled environment of a phone call where you can focus purely on voice and content. Still others benefit from the considered pacing of written exchange. Different conversations work in different mediums - matching the channel to the pressure dynamics of what you're discussing.

You surface calm and energised rather than exhausted. You followed the fundamental diving principle - respect the pressure, equalise gradually, never force your way through resistance. Most importantly, you can return tomorrow to continue exploring, because you worked with pressure instead of against it.

What Really Matters:
Before diving into difficult conversations, equalise the pressure between your ears first.

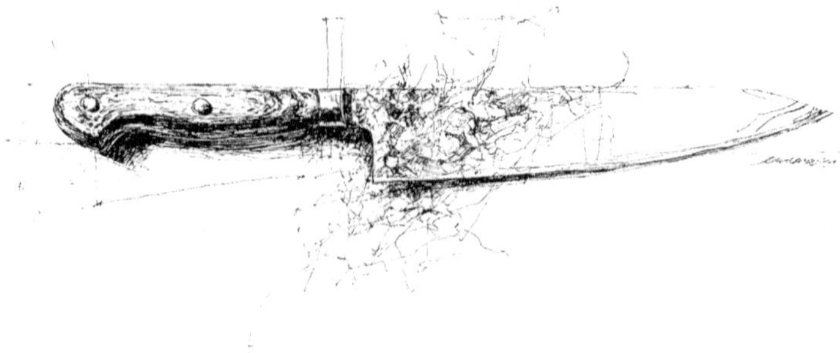

15

Trust

A foundation of relationships and functioning societies

Pick up a chef's knife from any professional kitchen. You'll feel something remarkable. The handle, dark with age and worn smooth, fits your grip perfectly. Not because it was carved that way, but because the chef's hands have shaped it over time. Where fingers naturally rest, the wood has developed gentle hollows. Where the thumb grips during precise chopping, a subtle groove has formed. What started as standard equipment has become something personal, shaped through years of daily use.

Trust doesn't work the way most people assume. It's not about making impressive promises or grand gestures designed to catch attention. Trust develops more like that knife handle. Small, repeated interactions that gradually shape something reliable. Each kept promise wears away uncertainty. Each consistent response creates smoother cooperation for the next interaction. Over time, working with someone you trust feels as natural as holding a familiar knife.

This wisdom travels deep through human history. In medieval Europe, guild masters understood that their most valuable asset wasn't their techniques or tools - it was their reputation for reliable work. A master carpenter's reputation took decades to build, one project after another. Clients didn't just hire his skill; they hired his predictable excellence. While guilds attempted to establish quality controls through marking systems, customers often relied more on individual craftsmen's proven track records than on formal guild oversight.[23]

Across the ancient Mediterranean, Roman long-distance trade relied on reputation networks and banking services that enabled transactions across ports such as Alexandria and Ephesus.[24] A trader's reputation preceded him to every new port because decades of honoured agreements had worn his name smooth in the minds of foreign bankers. When his ships arrived, harbour masters knew exactly what to expect. Trust became something like portable currency, more valuable than gold because it opened doors that money alone could not.

When people decide whether to rely on someone, three unconscious questions run through their minds.[25] Can you do this? Will you bother to do it properly? And do you care what happens to me if you don't? These assessments of ability, benevolence and integrity get answered by your track record before you speak. People tend to bet on patterns, not potential.

Cathy learned this when she took over a failing community project in Leeds. The previous coordinator had made sweeping promises about funding and partnerships that never materialised. Instead of announcing ambitious plans, Cathy promised exactly three things: meeting notes within 24 hours, responses to questions within two working days and room setup completed a quarter of an hour before each session. That was it. Like a chef slowly wearing grooves into a knife handle through daily work, Cathy began building new patterns others could count on. Within about eight weeks, people started arriving early and volunteering without being asked.

But trust isn't just about competence - it fractures differently depending on why it breaks. When Cathy occasionally missed her 24-hour deadline because she lacked information or got overwhelmed, people understood. These were competence gaps. Research on trust repair shows that competence-based violations respond well to apology plus corrective action: acknowledge the gap, fix the system, show how you'll catch it next time.[26] But when the previous coordinator had made promises he never intended to keep, that was character. Character damage requires proving your values through consistent action over time and some relationships need distance rather than repair.

Trust builds gradually but shatters suddenly. Research across psychology demonstrates that negative events carry more weight than positive ones - a principle that explains why trust built over years can crack with one careless moment.[27] The people who understand this protect their reliability like chefs protect their favourite knives - not perfectly, but carefully, knowing that what took years to develop can fracture quickly from lapses.

The deeper pattern appears everywhere you look. Institutions earn trust through fair process and consistent enforcement rather than just transparency. Online, we navigate misinformation by checking multiple independent sources rather than relying on superficial markers like professional design or official-sounding names. In communities, bridging trust across different groups requires different skills than bonding trust within tight circles. The same principle applies: reliability patterns, built through repeated interactions, matter more than impressive claims.

In a world where everyone overpromises and under-delivers, simply doing what you say becomes a practical advantage. Research on trust in complex systems reveals that when overpromising is common, consistency creates competitive differentiation.[28] People notice consistency more than ambition. They trust predictable excellence over brilliant flashes. And once you've built that steady rhythm of small promises kept, everything else becomes possible.

What Really Matters:
Trust isn't manufactured - it's patiently shaped by consistent use.

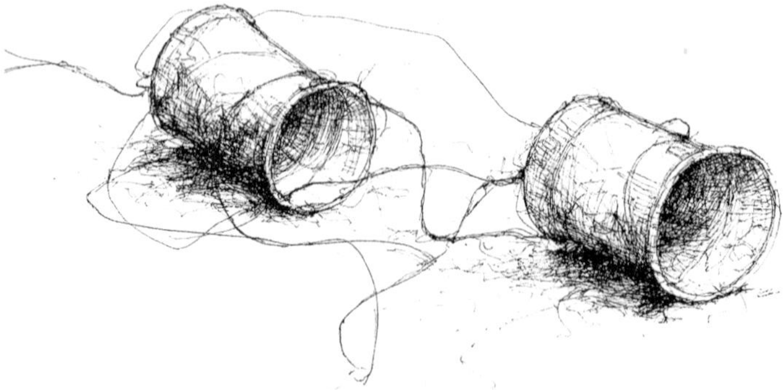

16

Interpersonal Conflict

Managing disagreements effectively

Elizabeth stands in her kitchen at 9 pm listening to the same frustrating argument for the third time. Holiday plans, miscommunication, hurt feelings. Her husband's words sliding past her explanations and hers past his. Each sentence makes less sense than the last, despite both of them speaking the same language.

Imaging two children playing with an old cup and string phone in the garden. When the string goes slack, their voices become garbled. But watch what they do when the line goes dead - they don't keep shouting into empty air. One calls out "hold on!" They both step back, pull the string taut with careful attention, before speaking again. Clear words can now travel the distance between them.

Elizabeth's kitchen argument works the same way. The problem isn't what they're saying - it's the communication line between them. When the line goes slack with interruption or rigid with defensiveness, nothing meaningful can get through. The repair is not to find the perfect words but learning to reset the line like the children did.

This insight reaches back through centuries of human wisdom. The South African philosophy of ubuntu - the principle that emphasises our shared humanity and interconnectedness - developed practices for heated disputes that followed a clear rhythm: make space, listen fully, then respond.[29] When emotions run high, you need to restore the connection first, then speak your truth.

Back in Elizabeth's kitchen, what she doesn't realise is that James's nervous system has kicked into a heightened stress state. When you're physiologically flooded during conflict, your heart rate spikes and it becomes much harder to take perspective or problem-solve.[30] His breathing has quickened. In this state, perspective-taking and problem-solving are much less available.

This is why cleverer arguments won't work anymore. Research on couples shows that when both partners are in this heightened state, their ability to process information, consider alternatives and solve problems together deteriorates markedly.[31] The body is prepared for fight or flight, not negotiation. Taking a break and returning once calmer often helps partners regain the capacity for actual resolution.[32]

"I need twenty minutes," Elizabeth says suddenly, recognising the futility. She walks to the local shop, buys a bottle of milk they don't need and lets her heart rate settle. When she returns, the room feels different. The line between them has gone slack, but now she knows how to pull it taut again.

"I'm sorry. You wanted us to check with your mum before booking anything and I went ahead without doing so," she begins, giving his point of view its fair hearing before adding her own. "That must have felt like I was ignoring you." He nods, tension leaving his face. The connection is now restored. A space opens for actual problem-solving instead of mutual defence.

The Jewish practice of teshuvah - acknowledging harm and taking responsibility to restore relationships - captures something essential about healing.[33] Research on effective apologies echoes this: name what you did, accept responsibility without hedging and offer one concrete action you'll take.[34] Elizabeth continues: "I felt defensive when you questioned the dates and I should have paused to understand why this mattered to you. I'll call the hotel to change the dates like your mum suggested."

The conversation that follows isn't about who was right but about how they'll navigate similar decisions together in future. They agree not to book family holidays without discussing together first. Small, practical boundaries that protect the connection they're learning to tend.

Not every line deserves to be repaired. Where there's ongoing coercion, threats or refusal to change harmful patterns, wisdom lies in distance and specialist support.[35][36] Forgiveness can happen privately for your own peace without requiring you to rebuild contact. The distinction matters: forgiveness relates to your inner stance towards past harm, while reconciliation requires safety and demonstrated change from the other person.[37] When you recognise patterns of harm, the cup and string phone metaphor shifts - sometimes the healthiest choice is to set down your end of the string entirely.

What Really Matters:
Pull the line taut with attention, then speak.

17

Community & Hospitality

Belonging, contribution and welcoming others

Picture a table set for six with seven chairs. The extra seat isn't a mistake - it's a statement. Someone has designed space for the person who isn't there yet. That empty chair changes the entire gathering. It signals that belonging gets built in, not left to chance. It says we expect you before we know you.

Ancient Greeks built this principle into their civilisation through xenia - sacred host-guest friendship under Zeus's protection.[38] The framework operated through clear protocols. When a stranger appeared at your door, you welcomed them inside, offered food and water and asked no questions until they had eaten. Only after they were fed and rested would you ask who they were or what they needed. The guest, in turn, respected household rules and would offer hospitality when your paths crossed again.

The protocols worked because structure enabled openness. The host knew what to offer. The stranger knew what to expect. Clear frameworks - food before questions, respect before familiarity - created safety for genuine connection between people who shared no history, no language, no certainty about each other's intentions. The boundaries didn't restrict hospitality. They made it possible.

This design principle appears in how spaces either welcome or exclude. A neighbourhood book club meets weekly in someone's living room. Eight regular members, comfortable routines. Then someone places an extra chair in the circle and puts a small sign by the door: "Book lovers welcome - ask inside for details." Within weeks, the circle grows to fifteen but more importantly the conversation changes. New voices ask questions the original members never considered. Books they'd never heard of appear on the reading list. The empty chair didn't just add people - it transformed what the group could see.

Research on isolation and belonging reveals why the principle matters. Isolation triggers stress responses similar to physical pain. The same neural regions that process physical injury also process social exclusion.[39] Stronger social relationships associate with better health and survival.[40] The empty chair works both ways. The stranger gains belonging. The community gains perspective, resilience, renewal.

But designing the empty chair requires attention to thresholds. Cafés that thrive make crossing easier through visible choices: clear signs about where to order and sit, menus that explain themselves, staff who notice when someone looks uncertain.[41] The design answers questions before they become barriers Where do I belong in this space? What do I do first? Who can I ask?

The empty chair also means giving people something to contribute. Bring-and-share suppers operate on this principle - everyone brings a dish, no one leaves hungry. The approach treats every newcomer as someone with something to offer. Sports clubs that hand first-timers equipment to try. Community groups that give newcomers a small, bounded task within the first meeting - timekeeper, note-taker, door greeter. The empty chair becomes a participant's chair through designed pathways from arrival to contribution.[42]

Clear frameworks enable all of this. The Greek protocols balanced generous hospitality with clear expectations. You knew your role as guest. You knew your obligations as host. The framework created safety for openness. Without structure, welcome becomes chaos and the stranger doesn't know how to enter. The community doesn't know how to receive. The empty chair sits unused not from lack of goodwill but from lack of design.

What Really Matters:
Design space for the stranger and you strengthen the entire social fabric.

18

Ethics & Altruism

Principles for treating others well and giving

Think of the last time someone helped you when they didn't have to. The neighbour who brought your bins in while you were away. The friend who remembered something you mentioned weeks earlier and followed up. The stranger who gave you directions when you were lost. You probably remember exactly how it felt. What you might not realise is that these moments work like seeds.

Treating others well isn't sacrifice - it's cultivation that compounds. We treat generosity as loss, as if kindness depletes us. But communities where people help each other develop stronger bonds and weather crises better. Organisations where people feel genuinely cared for show stronger cooperation and lower staff turnover.[44] Care creates the trust that makes everything else possible.

Ethical behaviour works like tending a garden. Every fair dealing, every kept promise, every moment of genuine attention plants seeds in the social soil around you. Some sprout within weeks - the customer who stays loyal, the colleague who helps you later. Others lie dormant for months before growing into opportunities you never expected. You can't control exactly what grows or when, but gardens cultivated with consistent care develop ecosystems that support the gardener.

In Hindu and Buddhist philosophy, karma captures how actions ripple forward through time - not as cosmic punishment, but as cause and effect in human relationships. When you treat someone with respect or cruelty, you set in motion chains of response that shape the social world you inhabit.[45] Ancient Roman patrons understood this practically. When they provided housing, legal support and business introductions to younger people starting out, they built bonds of mutual obligation that strengthened both parties for decades. Someone helped early in life often became their patron's strongest ally later.[46]

The sociologist Alvin Gouldner discovered that reciprocity operates as a fundamental norm across cultures: we remember who treats us well and feel moved to return the favour.[47] The challenge comes from expecting gardens to work like vending machines. You want immediate returns. But gardens don't reward on that schedule. You plant in spring for autumn harvest. You nurture soil that feeds plants you haven't chosen yet. The reward arrives later than you planned, often in forms you didn't expect, but it compounds.

Watch what happens when someone takes responsibility for a mistake that wasn't entirely theirs. A project deadline gets missed. They could blame their colleague who'd been struggling with a family crisis. Instead, they tell the manager "I should have caught this earlier" and work late to fix it. Three months pass. Then promotion time arrives, and that colleague writes the strongest recommendation anyone has seen. The person who helped didn't calculate future returns. They just knew covering for someone in crisis was right. The garden grew anyway.

When people know you'll treat them fairly even when it costs you something, they invest more in cooperation.[48] When they see you keep promises under pressure, they're willing to make agreements that benefit everyone. The person who helps a stranger or supports someone's education doesn't lose resources - they gain networks, goodwill and opportunities that often repay the effort over time.[49]

When we trust people to know what they need most, unconditional support often proves more effective than heavily conditional programmes. People who receive unconditional cash transfers typically invest in education, housing improvements and small business development. These choices reflect their actual circumstances better than external assumptions could.[50]

Setting boundaries works the same way. Saying no to requests that would drain you preserves your capacity to say yes to what matters. A clear boundary plants seeds of respect and prevents the resentment that kills relationships. People learn they can trust you to be honest about your limits, which makes it more meaningful when you do say yes.

The 18th-century philosopher Adam Smith wrote that we naturally desire "not only to be loved, but to be lovely."[51] The garden you tend through ethical behaviour - fair dealing, kept promises, genuine care - becomes the source of your strongest relationships, your best opportunities and your deepest satisfaction. Not because you're gaming the system, but because you're working with how human cooperation actually develops.

What Really Matters:
Ethics isn't sacrifice - it's tending the garden of the life you actually want.

19

Justice & Power

How fairness works and authority operates

In the final minutes of a crucial match, a referee makes a controversial call. The crowd erupts. Players protest. What separates a referee who keeps control from one who loses it entirely is explanation. The referee who points to the rulebook, shows what they saw, and applies the same standards to both teams gets far less grief than one who simply blows the whistle without any explanation.[52] Players might hate individual calls, but they keep playing because they understand the game is bigger than any single moment. The rules are visible, consistent, and fairly applied.

This is legitimacy in action - the mysterious quality that lets some people make tough decisions while others can't get anyone to follow simple instructions. The difference isn't having the final word. It's helping people understand how that word gets decided.

During Cathy's first year managing a community health clinic, funding cuts meant eliminating Saturday morning walk-in hours that served dozens of families without regular doctors. The numbers didn't lie - they had to make cuts. But Cathy knew how much this would hurt people. She called a public meeting and shared the actual budget numbers. She walked everyone through alternatives she'd considered and why each was impossible, then gave residents twenty minutes to respond before finalising anything. The cuts happened anyway. But instead of furious voicemails and angry petitions, she got reluctant nods and people brainstorming ways to raise money. They understood she was stuck between a rock and a hard place. So instead of shooting the messenger, they rolled up their sleeves and started thinking about solutions.

The pattern appears across centuries. In medieval England, Henry II inherited a kingdom drowning in arbitrary local justice. Before Henry, each powerful lord made up rules as he went along - one village might hang someone for theft while the next village over imposed a fine for the same crime.[53] Punishments varied wildly depending on who you knew and how much you could pay. Henry came up with something brilliant - but it wasn't quite what you'd expect. Instead of making punishments harsher, he made them more predictable. He sent judges around the country who had to follow the same royal rules wherever they went - one set of laws for all of England. Plus, everything had to be written down, and judges had to explain their reasoning.[54] No more making it up as you go along. This "common law" didn't eliminate harsh outcomes, but it made them explainable. For the first time, ordinary people could grasp how justice worked.

Back in Rome, centuries earlier, Marcus Tullius Cicero - Rome's most famous lawyer and politician - would rise to defend clients in packed courthouses. Winning or losing wasn't the point, it was what he did next that mattered. He would walk the room through every piece of law that applied. He quoted the precedents. He even gave his opponent's arguments a fair hearing before he started picking them apart, piece by piece, with hard evidence.[55] By the time he was done, everyone in that room - whether they liked his client or not - knew exactly how he reached his conclusion. Two thousand years later, we still read those speeches not because Cicero always won, but because he showed how justice works when it works properly. Through reasons anyone can follow, rules that apply to everyone, and processes that give dignity to all sides.

Other societies experienced this too. Islamic legal scholars developed rigorous methods for interpreting religious law precisely to prevent judges from making things up based on personal whims.[56] Chinese imperial administrators established detailed protocols for hearing citizen complaints - a recognition that unexplained decisions breed rebellion.[57]

These societies developed practices around something fundamental about human psychology. We have a deep need for fair process that goes beyond getting what we want.[58] We'll accept outcomes that hurt us if we believe the process was legitimate. But we'll fight beneficial decisions if they feel arbitrary or rigged. This goes deeper than just how we're raised. It's baked into how humans work together.

The principle matters more urgently now as algorithms increasingly shape our lives - loan approvals, job applications, benefit eligibility, even criminal sentencing recommendations. The danger isn't just hidden bias, though that's genuine enough. It's decisions without reasons anyone can grasp or challenge.[59] When a computer system rejects your mortgage application, you need the same thing Cicero's clients got in that Roman courthouse: an explanation of what rules were applied, what evidence was considered, and how to appeal if something went wrong.

What Really Matters:
People follow authority they can understand, even when they hate the decisions.

20

Cultural Navigation

Managing difference when systems meet

The German engineer arrived at nine sharp, as the meeting invite specified. By 9:15, only two of the seven Italian colleagues had appeared. By 9:30, when the full group had assembled and were greeting each other warmly over espresso, he was visibly frustrated. To him, punctuality showed respect for everyone's time and professional commitment. To them, gathering the right people and building rapport before diving into business showed respect for relationships and the work itself. Neither side was being difficult. It's simply like driving on different sides of the road - both approaches work brilliantly until they crash together at a junction.

Think of culture as traffic rules that keep social interaction flowing smoothly. In Britain you keep left, in France you keep right. Every detail becomes second nature once you know the local rules. The system is largely invisible until something goes wrong. Then suddenly you notice how much coordination was happening beneath your awareness.[60]

Cultural crashes happen at the junction, not on the open road. When different systems meet without clear guidance about which rules apply, small moves stop being obvious. A direct question can feel refreshingly honest in one context and brutally aggressive in another.[61] The person whose behaviour baffles you isn't being difficult - they're following rules that worked perfectly in their cultural neighbourhood.

Ancient Chinese thinkers understood this problem deeply. In classical Confucian thought, li refers to ritual propriety - a choreography of gestures, timing and responses that coordinates social interaction and preserves everyone's dignity.[62] Think of it as visible traffic rules for relationships. A raised eyebrow might signal mild interest in one cultural context and serious disapproval in another. Li creates explicit choreography so everyone knows what each gesture means. When someone from outside doesn't know the steps, you adapt the choreography for the moment so everyone can participate without embarrassment.[63]

This matters because underneath all cultural difference sit familiar psychological patterns. People sort the world into us and them remarkably quickly - watch any office cafeteria at lunchtime and you'll see the same tables filling with the same groups, an efficient habit that once helped our ancestors distinguish friend from stranger.[64] Within groups, much goes unsaid. Between colleagues who've worked together for years, a raised eyebrow or slight pause communicates volumes.

Across groups, those same signals become invisible. What feels obviously polite to you carries that feeling because you learned these particular traffic rules from the people who raised you-Communication styles vary in how much they rely on shared background. High-context communication packs meaning into tone, timing and what's left unsaid - common in cultures where people grow up in tight-knit communities. Low-context communication spells things out explicitly in words - common where people regularly interact with strangers.[60] Neither approach is superior. They're simply different traffic systems that collide when they meet without clear signals.

Research on contact between different cultural groups shows that interaction can reduce prejudice, especially when status is roughly equal, goals are shared and someone with clear authority backs the cooperation.[65] Without these elements, contact can harden existing biases as people misinterpret unfamiliar behaviours through their own cultural lens.

A software company found this out when an American manager publicly praised a Japanese developer in the quarterly review meeting, singling him out for exceptional code quality that had accelerated the project. The manager expected this recognition would motivate both the individual and the team. Instead, the developer looked distressed, and his teammates grew noticeably quieter in subsequent meetings. The manager was baffled - surely acknowledging excellence was universal? But in his team member's cultural framework, being singled out broke group harmony and made colleagues lose face by comparison. Success belonged to the team, not the individual. Once the manager understood the junction, he started framing achievements collectively: "The backend team delivered this ahead of schedule" rather than "Kenji's exceptional work saved us two weeks." Same appreciation, different traffic signals that preserved group cohesion.

The pattern that works: name the junction rather than blame the drivers. When cultural confusion hits, someone asks "What rule are you following here?" Signs get adjusted to fit the actual group present. People can switch approaches without losing face.

Important limits apply though. Not every collision is harmless misunderstanding - some cultural rules systematically exclude people, and that's unfair regardless of tradition. The test is simple: does this rule help everyone's traffic flow safely, or does it block some people while letting others through?

Belonging develops when we attend to basic human needs for inclusion and fair treatment.[66] This isn't about grand gestures or cultural festivals. It's about managing the intersections. Make different systems visible, adjust signs honestly when they're not working, and remember that confusion happens because of poor signalling, not malicious intent.

What Really Matters:
Manage the junction, not the drivers. Cultural difference is a coordination problem, not a character problem.

Part 3

The World & Beyond

Beyond the Human Circle

The relationships you've built - with yourself, with others, with your communities - don't exist in isolation. They're embedded in larger systems that shape every aspect of human experience. The food you share comes from agricultural networks spanning continents. The tools you use extend human capabilities in ways previous generations couldn't imagine. The stories you tell draw from millennia of cultural wisdom and are now being joined by new forms of intelligence that process information differently than any human mind.

These wider contexts - ecological, economic, technological - are changing faster than ever before. Understanding your place within them becomes essential for navigating what comes next. These themes move from the natural foundations we depend on, through the human systems we've built, to the meaning-making that defines our place in the larger story.

21

Nature

Our relationship with the living world

You sit at a pottery wheel, hands muddy and slippery, completely frustrated. For the third time this morning, your clay has collapsed. You keep trying to force it into the bowl you've pictured, pushing harder when it resists, gripping tighter when it starts to wobble. The approach isn't working.

The clay teaches you what it wants to become. You can't impose your vision on resistant material. Instead, you feel how wet it is today, how much sand is mixed in, where it wants to give and where it holds firm. You work with the clay's nature, not against it. Push too hard and it collapses. Work with its grain and suddenly you're partners in making something neither of you could create alone. This pattern - caring preceding understanding, hands learning before minds grasp - appears in how humans relate to living systems.

Aldo Leopold, who became one of America's most influential conservationists, discovered it as a young forester in the American Southwest. In 1909, he shot a wolf and watched what he later called the fierce green fire die in its eyes - a moment that shattered something.[1] Leopold had believed good stewardship meant controlling nature. Killing predators, maximising timber yields, treating forest as material to be shaped by force. But that wolf's death started a decades-long shift in his thinking. He began watching how ecosystems actually worked: what happened when you removed predators, how different species depended on each other, where human intervention helped and where it destroyed. His land ethic emerged from years of careful observation: "We abuse land because we regard it as a commodity belonging to us. When we see land as a community to which we belong, we may begin to use it with love and respect."[1] The forester had become a listener.

The Menominee Nation, a Native American tribe in Wisconsin, developed a sustained version of this partnership. Since 1856, the tribe has sustained timber harvests whilst substantially increasing standing timber.[2] Chief Oshkosh's guidance shaped their approach: "Start with the rising sun and work toward the setting sun, but take only the mature trees, the sick trees, and the trees that have fallen."[3] This wasn't romantic primitivism - it worked. Hemlock and cedar are indicators of forest health: they're shade-tolerant species that thrive in mature, stable forests but struggle in damaged ones. Recent ecological studies show Menominee forests contain over five times more hemlock seedlings and twice as many cedar seedlings as nearby national forests, meaning their forests are healthier and regenerating naturally.[4] They also have higher overall tree volume, greater plant diversity, and fewer invasive species.How do they do it? They combine traditional observation with modern forestry: continuous inventory tracking shows what each forest stand needs, selective harvesting removes only what benefits the whole and they pay attention to what the forest reveals about its own health. Their hands grew sensitive to what the land was telling them.

Like hands growing sensitive to clay, sustained contact changes what you notice. A regular walk through the same park reveals patterns: which plants stress in summer heat, where water pools after rain, what birds appear when. Awareness picks up signals that were always there.[5]

This pattern transforms urban planning and habitat restoration. Cities that restore river corridors and add green infrastructure can reduce urban heat.[6] Rain gardens handle stormwater whilst supporting pollinators. Community food gardens feed neighbourhoods whilst building soil. The approach doesn't mean abandoning human needs. Potters shape clay, they don't just admire it. But shaping works by understanding properties, working with strengths, respecting limits.

Clay that seems impossible one day becomes responsive the next, not because you've mastered some technique, but because your hands have learned to listen. That patch of degraded land behind your neighbourhood might look hopeless now, but consistent tending - the patient attention of a craftsperson - often reveals possibilities no one expected. The learning can't be rushed.

What Really Matters:
Nature works like clay - feel what it needs, respect its limits, let contact teach care.

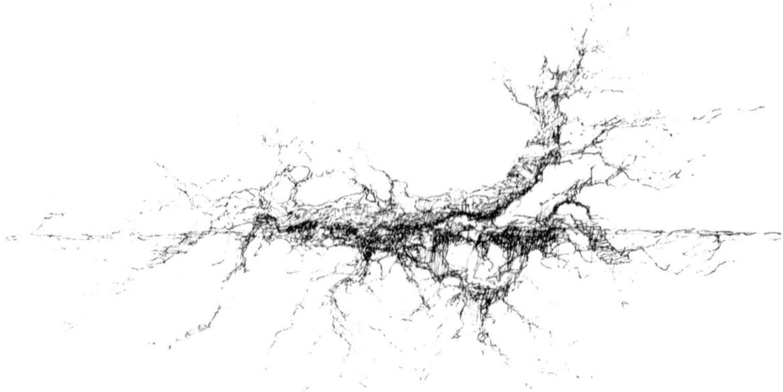

22

Food & Agriculture

Growing, sharing and the cultures around food

You can't see the real internet that feeds the world. It's happening right now beneath your feet - billions of connections pulsing through soil, trading nutrients and information along pathways finer than human hair. Fungal networks stretch between plant roots like fibre optic cables, sharing sugars, phosphorus and chemical signals.[7] This underground network has ancient origins, and it operates on a simple principle that transformed agriculture once humans figured it out: cooperation beats competition.

Across civilisations, farmers observed patterns in the land. Certain crop sequences restored fertility. Fields planted with beans one year grew better wheat the next.[8] What they couldn't see was the fungal internet connecting plant roots or that legumes could pull nitrogen from the air and feed it to the soil. But they trusted what worked and built farming systems around these partnerships.

What these farmers learned was that forcing the land into simplicity always backfires eventually. The soil internet thrives on diversity. Healthy soil teems with organisms trading services in an economy more complex than any stock exchange - bacteria, fungi and countless tiny creatures all exchanging nutrients and information.[9] When we plough diverse landscapes into single-crop fields, we're essentially cutting the cables. The network crashes[9] and suddenly we need to import everything - fertiliser, pesticides, even the basic biological processes that used to run themselves.

Three years ago, a farmer's fields were like a bad internet connection - patchy, unreliable, expensive to maintain. One hot July he knelt down and examined the soil closely. Where he'd been planting only wheat, the earth was compacted and lifeless. But along the field margins, where wildflowers had established, the soil felt different - crumbly, alive, full of channels and air pockets. He realised he'd been thinking about his farm like a factory when he should have been thinking like a network engineer.

The transformation took two growing seasons to become clear. Where diverse plantings were allowed and hedgerows established, pest problems found natural solutions. Beneficial insects moved in from the flower strips. Root systems explored deeper, finding water during dry spells. Fungal partnerships began reconnecting across the field. More diversified farming systems produce more stable yields across varying weather conditions.[10] Not necessarily higher peaks, but reliable harvests when conditions get difficult. The insight wasn't chasing peak yields in perfect years. It was maintaining the biological networks that deliver resilience when weather throws curveballs.

Traditional farming systems embody this principle: resilience comes from relationships, not inputs.[11] Andean farmers developed potato varieties that could survive at different altitudes precisely because they understood soil as community rather than commodity. Chinese farmers created systems where fish, ducks and rice all shared the same space, turning waste from each organism into food for another - closed loops that fed more people from less land. Food cultures worldwide embed this same pattern: intercropping beans with corn and squash, integrating livestock into crop rotations, maintaining seed varieties adapted to local conditions. These aren't romantic gestures - they're biological network engineering at landscape scale.

What Really Matters:
The soil internet runs on cooperation, not competition - and that's the blueprint our food systems need.

23

Sustainability

Balancing present needs with future possibilities

Daphne stands in her empty backyard holding a tiny apple sapling, feeling slightly ridiculous. The tree is barely three feet tall, no thicker than her thumb and cost her £45 - more than a day's pension. Her neighbour leans over the fence with a smirk: "You know that thing won't give you shade for twenty years, right? Why not just buy a patio umbrella?" But something - maybe stubbornness, maybe the thought of her grandchildren Luke and Sonia picking apples here someday - makes her dig the hole anyway. In that moment of planting, she discovers the pattern that reshapes how we think about every choice we make.

Daphne is tying up her time, money and a corner of her yard in something that offers no immediate return. For years, this tree will demand water, protection and patience while giving back almost nothing visible. Yet by accepting these limits now, she creates possibilities no immediate purchase could match.

Traditional cultures understood this temporal trade-off intuitively. Across Islamic societies from medieval times onwards, donors created waqf - charitable endowments - so their property could keep helping people indefinitely. A merchant might endow an orchard or farmland, with its yield feeding a local soup kitchen or school and a portion reserved for upkeep and replanting so the asset renews itself. These trusts bound future generations to sustain what their founders would never see flourish.[12] They chose to forgo immediate gains to ensure plenty for descendants they would never meet. Japan's hanami tradition - the centuries-old practice of celebrating cherry blossoms - began with rulers planting thousands of cherry trees that later generations enjoy. Across medieval Europe, communities managed woodlands under systems that limited immediate use to preserve resources for the future.[13] Different times and places, same discovery: the deepest freedom comes from choosing the right limitations early.

For the first few years, all the tree's energy goes into invisible work - establishing roots, strengthening its core, learning to read the soil and seasons. Nothing shows above ground but slow, patient growth. But once those foundations are secure, something remarkable happens. The tree doesn't just grow - it transforms into abundance. Branches spread wide, creating cool shade on hot days. Leaves produce oxygen and filter the air. Eventually, it will feed her grandchildren with crisp apples for decades. What looked like a limitation in those early years becomes the foundation for decades of gifts the tree gives freely. Earth's resources work the same way. You cannot spend carbon or materials twice; Earth's accounts must balance, just like any household budget.

The same pattern appears at every scale. Countries that planted their energy futures early now harvest the returns. Denmark invested heavily in wind power in the 1970s when it was expensive and uncertain - the equivalent of planting trees that wouldn't bear fruit for decades. Denmark has one of the highest wind shares among IEA members, with low power-sector carbon intensity and strong interconnectors.[14] Costa Rica chose forest protection and restoration over short-term logging profits in the 1980s. Forest cover roughly doubled between the late 1980s and 2010s under payments for ecosystem services and protection policies.[15]

Daphne learns that accepting some limits now isn't sacrifice - it's investing in lasting wealth. When she switches to filtered tap water instead of buying bottled water, she's not giving up convenience. She's making a choice that typically cuts plastic waste and, in places with safe municipal supplies, usually costs less over time.[16] Well-designed and properly installed insulation cuts heating and cooling needs and improves comfort, with savings that vary by home and climate.[17] Expanding renewables and efficiency reduces exposure to fossil-fuel import volatility and strengthens energy security over time.[18]

Communities that invest in infrastructure discover this pattern too. When Daphne's community chooses bike lanes over more parking, they're planting infrastructure that gives people more transportation choices, cleaner air and healthier lives for decades.[19] When they invest in public transport instead of wider highways, they're constraining immediate convenience but planting the seeds of liveable cities.[20]

The insight is learning which choices create lasting value and which just waste resources. Daphne could have spent her tree money on something that gave immediate pleasure but disappeared quickly. Instead, she invested in something that would grow in value year after year. Every sustainability choice follows the same pattern - using less today creates plenty tomorrow, building for durability creates lasting satisfaction, thinking beyond ourselves creates a world our children will thank us for.

What Really Matters:
The shade you sit in tomorrow comes from a tree you plant today.

24

Technology & Tools

Extensions of human capabilities and their effects

Try navigating without GPS, banking without online access, staying connected without messaging apps, or managing work without email. It's almost impossible to live without technology. What feels like dependence today began as convenience yesterday. Take James, for example. When he wakes up, the first thing he does is reach for his phone. This habit is no longer really a choice. It all started simply enough - he used his phone as an alarm clock. But somewhere along the way, without him noticing, the terms of his relationship with his phone evolved. What began as a helpful wake-up call became daily infrastructure for his life. His phone became both his external memory and constant companion. The phone didn't force this shift - it simply made new behaviours possible, then gradually made them necessary.

This is what happens when we adopt any significant tool or technology. We enter an invisible handshake. The tool offers capability; we offer it our attention and dependency. Both sides benefit at first, but the terms shift over time.

The handshake begins innocently. A GPS helps you navigate unfamiliar streets. A calculator speeds up arithmetic. A search engine finds information faster than any library. Each tool extends your natural abilities - the hammer becomes part of your arm, the screen part of your visual field.[21] Your brain incorporates these objects as extensions of yourself.

But the invisible handshake changes its terms without renegotiating. As the tool becomes reliable, your own capabilities can begin to weaken from disuse.[22] London taxi drivers build enlarged brain regions through years of navigation practice.[23] But when people follow turn-by-turn directions, the brain parts responsible for building mental maps show reduced activity during navigation tasks.[24] The tool that was supposed to enhance your ability can gradually start to replace it instead.

James knows this pattern from his own experience. For years, he knew his city well - the back routes, the shortcuts, which roads flooded in heavy rain. He'd driven these streets for work, building a detailed mental map without thinking about it. When he first got GPS, he used it sensibly enough: checking traffic before long journeys, finding addresses in unfamiliar suburbs. Gradually, though, he began switching it on for every trip. It was just easier. The app knew the traffic; it rerouted around delays; it told him exactly when he'd arrive. His navigation skills weren't deliberately abandoned - they simply faded through disuse. Now, five years later, James finds himself lost without the voice in his dashboard. Even in his own neighbourhood, he'll turn on the GPS rather than trust his memory. The handshake shifted: the tool maintained his mobility while quietly eroding the very skill that made him confident on the road.

Network effects multiply the handshake's power. When enough people adopt WhatsApp, not having it means missing important communications.[25] When calculators are everywhere, mental arithmetic skills matter less. The tool doesn't just change you - it changes the world around you, making alternatives less practical.

This process follows predictable patterns. What seems optional soon becomes expected, what feels like enhancement quickly becomes necessity.[26] The switching costs rise steadily - learning new interfaces, rebuilding habits, accepting reduced capability - making it harder to change course.[25]

Once established, these handshakes become difficult to break. Think of the QWERTY keyboard. It was designed to stop the metal typebars in old typewriters from jamming when common letter pairs were typed quickly - but we're all still using it today, long after those mechanical constraints disappeared.[27] Breaking this handshake would require collective coordination that rarely happens outside of a crisis.

The invisible handshake isn't inherently bad. Many tools genuinely improve human capability without significant trade-offs.[28] Eyeglasses extend vision; bicycles multiply movement efficiency; books preserve knowledge across time. The question isn't whether to shake hands with technology - we've been doing that since the first stone tools. The question is whether the terms remain balanced.

The most sustainable handshakes maintain some symmetry - the tool enhances capability without completely replacing it. Professional chefs use sharp knives but know how to work with basic tools; musicians use amplifiers but can still play acoustically; architects use CAD software but maintain their sketching skills. The London taxi drivers offer a template: they use GPS for traffic updates but navigate primarily through their mental maps. They've shaken hands with the technology while maintaining their core competency. When the GPS fails or gives poor directions, they're not stranded.

What Really Matters:
Every tool offers an invisible handshake.

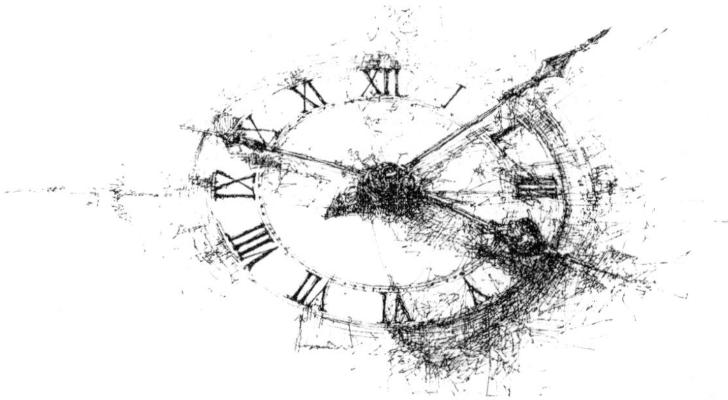

25

Money & Economics

How resources flow and create value

When you drink a cup of tea, you're completing a coordination sequence that began months ago. The price you paid was a timing signal that reached back through the supply chain - telling a smallholder farmer in Assam when to harvest, a blender in Sri Lanka what to create, a shipping network when to move containers across oceans. Your purchase didn't create this tea on demand. It synchronised human effort across continents and seasons, aligning work that happened months apart to arrive precisely when you needed it.

In March 2021, a container ship got stuck in the Suez Canal for six days. Tea shipments stalled. Container ships rerouted around South Africa, adding weeks to journey times. Space on ships became scarce, pushing prices upward. The rising prices were timing signals broadcasting backward through the supply chain: 'We need to adjust.' Within weeks, buyers shifted orders, suppliers modified schedules, and the system realigned itself around the disruption. No government committee met. No central planner issued orders. Millions of individual decisions, guided by changing prices, coordinated the global response.

This reveals a fundamental truth about how economic systems actually work. We think we're trading things - pounds for groceries, euros for petrol, dollars for rent. But we're aligning time. Money is humanity's most sophisticated technology for synchronising effort between strangers who will never meet, across distances and decades they'll never cross.

A rising tea price tells farmers 'plant more next season' without anyone needing to call them.[29] A falling price sends a different signal, redirecting effort elsewhere. Every price compresses countless individual decisions about what people want and what's available into a simple number that helps billions coordinate their actions across time.

Humanity has been perfecting this coordination technology for millennia. By around 200 CE, tea was already moving along Silk Road routes into Tibet and toward Central Asia, with caravans timing journeys by water and pasture availability.[30] The Tea Horse Road formalised coordination between harvest cycles and seasonal mountain passes.[31] The British East India Company scaled this to industrial proportions - by the 1830s, coordinating 30 million pounds in weight of tea annually across monsoon harvests, jungle transport and intercontinental shipping.[32] Each advance was learning how to align human efforts across greater distances and longer time spans through price signals.

Right now, wheat harvests in Kansas are being timed to bread consumption in Tokyo. Microchip fabrication in Taiwan is synchronised with phone assembly in China and purchase patterns in London. Oil extraction in the North Sea aligns with transport networks spanning continents. Software developers in Bangalore coordinate their coding schedules with startup needs in San Francisco. A steel worker in Sheffield times production to the car manufacturer's assembly line in Detroit. None of these people know each other. None requires a central coordinator. Price signals synchronise their efforts across time.

Saving isn't about accumulating numbers. It's storing the ability to tell the economy what to do later. Your savings account is a claim on future coordination. Investing means letting others use your timing signals now to build something valuable, promising to synchronise even more economic activity with your future needs. Both are technologies for coordinating effort across time.[33]

The system's effectiveness relies on collective trust in this coordination network. We accept timing signals today because we trust others will honour them tomorrow.[34] When inflation rises, the signals become unreliable - what you saved yesterday buys less tomorrow. If too many people lose faith at once, entire monetary systems can break down,[35] leaving individual efforts unable to connect with others' needs across time.

Modern technology amplifies coordination power dramatically.[36] You can tap Pay Now on your phone and trigger timing sequences spanning the globe - the components manufactured eighteen months ago, the software written last year, the assembly completed three months back. Digital payments move at the speed of light, but they're doing what Silk Road caravans did at three miles per hour: aligning past effort with present needs through price signals.

The technology also reveals stark inequalities. We do not all start with the same coordination power.[37] Some people inherit extensive financial power, while others are born with almost none. This inequality determines whose efforts get synchronised with whose needs and how quickly. Those with more money direct more human effort. Their timing signals reach further and trigger more coordination.

Step back and you see something extraordinary. Every purchase is a signal sent backward through time. Every price change ripples forward, redirecting future effort. Seasonal agricultural cycles synchronise with year-round urban consumption. Today's investments align with innovations that won't mature for decades. Supply chains spanning continents coordinate themselves through price signals, no central mind required.

Millions of strangers wake up each morning and guided by market signals, coordinate their efforts to create exactly what others need, when they need it. The system turns chaos into choreography. Millions of separate decisions become coordinated flow.

What Really Matters:
Money and economics synchronise time, not things.

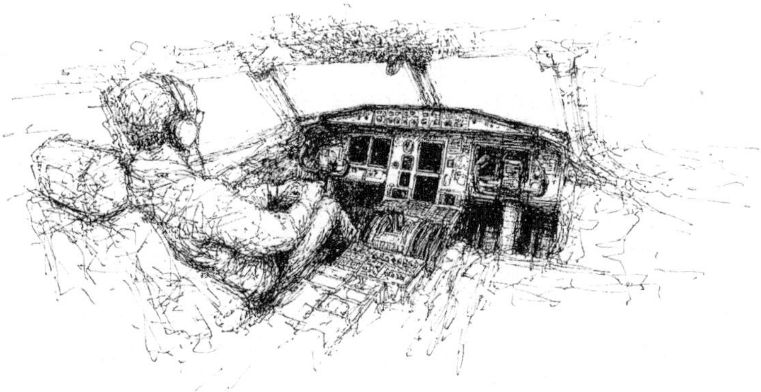

26

Story & Myth

Why we need narratives to make sense of the world

The fairytale goes like this. A clever rabbit tricks a fox into freeing him from a trap. Children hear it and giggle at the rabbit's cunning. Adults retell it and spot lessons about using wit when you're outmatched. Communities facing oppression discover it carries instructions for resistance - how the powerless can survive against overwhelming odds. Same story. Three completely different instruction manuals.

This is how stories work. We don't just read them or watch them - we run them like flight simulators. Characters become test pilots for choices we might face. Plot becomes the physics engine that shows what leads to what. When done well, stories let you rehearse difficult decisions with the safety on, building judgement without paying the real-world costs of poor choices.

When you read a vivid narrative, your mind activates the same neural networks used for actual perception and action.[38] Your brain runs a simulation of the experience, letting you practice responses to situations you may never have encountered. This is why a well-told story about making a difficult moral choice can improve your moral reasoning. Your brain treats the imagined scenario as rehearsal.

This simulator principle explains why narrative structure isn't just satisfying - it's survival equipment. Beginning-middle-end mirrors how your brain naturally segments experience into episodes.[39] Characters aren't decoration - they're the variables you test different approaches through. Causation isn't just plot mechanics - it's the feedback system showing which actions lead to which outcomes.

Around the 3rd century BCE, Indian scholars compiled the Panchatantra - a collection of animal fables created to train young princes in statecraft and practical wisdom.[42] A king worried his three sons were incompetent asked a scholar named Vishnusharma to transform them into capable rulers. Vishnusharma refused gold and created stories instead, claiming he could achieve in six months what formal instruction had failed to accomplish in years.

Each tale works on multiple levels. A child hearing about a crow dropping pebbles into a pitcher to raise the water level learns basic problem-solving - when you can't reach something directly, change the environment. An adolescent sees patterns about persistence. An administrator sees lessons about working within constraints. A ruler facing political opposition sees strategies for achieving goals without obvious power.

The monkey and crocodile story shows this clearly. A crocodile befriends a monkey, then tries to lure him into the river claiming his wife needs a monkey's heart to recover. The monkey, seeing the trap, claims he left his heart in a tree and must retrieve it. The crocodile carries him back to shore where he escapes. Surface lesson: don't trust those who suddenly change behaviour. Deeper: when trapped, quick thinking and understanding what the other person believes can save you. Deepest: the story shows how to buy time by working within someone else's assumptions while finding your exit.

What makes these stories work as simulators is compression. The Panchatantra doesn't lecture about alliance-building or managing betrayal - it shows these patterns through animals whose simple motivations make the underlying mechanics visible. A prince could run these scenarios mentally when facing real political situations.

The collection spread across Asia, the Middle East and eventually Europe, translated into dozens of languages. Each culture adapted the details while preserving the core mechanics. Persian translators made the stories more philosophical. Arabic versions emphasised moral instruction. European versions shifted toward individual ethics. But the function stayed constant: compressed scenarios that let readers rehearse responses to complex social situations.

The narrative structure of a story-simulator does the teaching. Your brain processes the sequence of events, tests interpretations, and extracts patterns you can apply to new situations. The explicit moral at the end serves as a bookmark. The real learning happens while running the simulation.

Research on how people process narratives confirms this pattern.[40] Readers build mental models of characters' goals and the world's cause-and-effect structure. They use these models to predict what happens next. Wrong predictions force the model to update. This is active learning through simulation, not passive information storage.

Digital platforms have turned the world into networked simulation rooms. One tap can push a story to millions in minutes. The hunger for story-based learning hasn't changed. The velocity has.

Short videos, interactive fiction, and viral narratives let millions rehearse choices together. Studies of information spread show that emotionally compelling stories often move faster than careful analysis.[41] A vivid simulation that fits what people already think will outrun a complex explanation that challenges them. This happens even when the explanation is more accurate. The pattern recognition system that helped stories transmit survival wisdom now operates at new speed and scale.

So how do you use stories as reliable simulators rather than just compelling fictions? You test their predictions against reality. When a story grabs you, notice what choice it's asking you to rehearse. What values does it encode? What would need to happen for you to change your mind about its central claim? What happens when you test its predictions against actual evidence? Stories that help you navigate reality hold up to this testing. Stories that help you avoid reality reveal their gaps when checked against the real world.

The Panchatantra has trained minds in practical reasoning for over two millennia because its patterns map onto recurring social dynamics. The specific crocodiles and monkeys are fictional, but the underlying mechanics - trust, betrayal, quick thinking under pressure, working within constraints - appear across every culture and era.

Stories remain humanity's most powerful learning technology because they feel like lived experience. Use them to expand your imagination and rehearse difficult decisions. But the most important skill in the age of infinite stories is knowing when to step out of the simulator and check how well its physics match the real world.

What Really Matters:
Stories are flight simulators for life choices - use them to practice decisions safely, then verify their lessons in the real world.

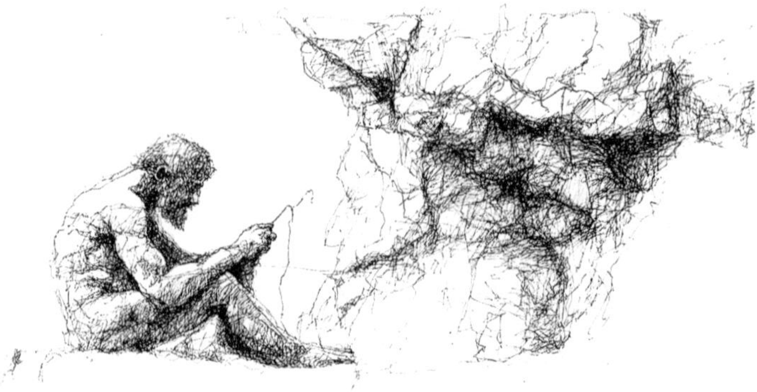

27

Art & Expression

How humans create and interpret meaning

Something subtle happens when art works. You enter a dark cave in southern France and suddenly you're standing 37,000 years in the past. Not because you're imagining it, but because someone working with torchlight and pigment on rough stone created something that still reaches across time to find you.

Between roughly 37,000 and 28,000 years ago, painters worked in the Chauvet caves with flickering flames.[43] They created horses that seem to gallop across the walls. They weren't just decorating. They were building a connection across three points that would hold for millennia: the maker's hand, the medium's properties and the audience's presence. Change any point and the whole relationship transforms.

The maker brought skill and intention to rough stone. The medium - cave walls with particular textures, pigments that caught the light, torches that made shadows dance - shaped what could be expressed. But meaning only emerged when someone entered that space, felt their breath catch. They understood they were seeing evidence of minds like their own reaching across time. The intersection of all three points created something none of them held alone.

This relationship keeps shifting. Ancient audiences entering by torchlight brought different understandings than modern visitors arriving with electric lamps and archaeological knowledge. The paintings haven't changed. The intersection has. It's an elastic triangle, if you want a phrase for it - three points in constant relation, where meaning lives not in any single corner but in the space between them all.

The same pattern appears 150 years later. In 1874, Claude Monet exhibited Impression, Sunrise at the first Impressionist exhibition in Paris. Critics saw loose brushwork, visible paint texture, colours that seemed unblended. Art critic Louis Leroy coined the term 'Impressionism' as mockery - these weren't finished paintings, just rough impressions.[44] The audience point of intersection demanded smooth, invisible brushstrokes. Monet's technique violated those expectations completely.

Today we stand before the same canvas and the intersection has transformed. Those loose brushstrokes now appear innovative, capturing the fleeting quality of light on water at sunrise. The visible paint texture feels expressive rather than crude. What 1874 audiences dismissed as sloppy technique, we now recognise as innovation that launched an entire movement. The maker and medium remained constant. The third point shifted, and with it, everything that emerged at their intersection.

The medium itself shapes what's possible at this intersection. A poem turns meaning into steps your eye must climb, line by line. A mural catches attention in public space, ambushing people who weren't looking for art. A performance puts ideas in motion through bodies moving in real time.[45] Each medium organises attention differently, creates different conditions for the intersection and makes different meanings possible.

This explains why interpretation isn't arbitrary even though it changes. Some readings account for all three points - what the maker actually did with form and material, how the medium shapes what can be felt and understood, what audiences bring to the encounter.[46] The strongest interpretations hold the whole intersection in view. Weak interpretations ignore one corner and collapse the space where meaning lives.

The most enduring art seems to recognise this from the start. It designs for the intersection rather than assuming meaning can be transmitted from one mind to another like a message in a bottle. It builds space for audiences bringing different backgrounds and ways of seeing. It allows for meanings to emerge that even the maker didn't anticipate. The relationship stays elastic because that's what lets art keep working across time, context and culture - not despite the changing points, but because of them.

What Really Matters:
Meaning in art emerges at the intersection of maker, medium and audience - and that intersection keeps changing.

28

Conflict, War & Peace

Understanding conflict and building stability

Two drivers round blind corners from opposite directions. Between them: a narrow bridge, barely wide enough for one vehicle. No time to brake safely, too much momentum to reverse. Rapidly, each driver calculates: the other looks hesitant, maybe young, probably inexperienced. Both press the accelerator, betting the other will swerve first. Neither does. The crash makes headlines, but the real tragedy isn't the collision itself. It's that both drivers made perfectly rational decisions based on incomplete information. And both were catastrophically wrong.

This is how most wars actually start. Not with ancient hatreds or irreconcilable differences, but with bad bets about who will blink first. The underlying disputes - territory, resources, religion, competing interests - often simmer for years or even decades. What transforms simmering tension into violence is the miscalculation: both sides betting the other will back down rather than fight. Leaders on both sides examine the evidence, consult advisors, weigh probabilities. Everyone concludes that a show of force will make the other side back down. The decision seems logical, even inevitable. Then both sides escalate simultaneously, each convinced they're calling the other's bluff, neither realising they're about to collide on the bridge.

Back in fifth-century Athens, the historian Thucydides watched this exact psychology destroy his world. The rivalry between Athens and Sparta had simmered for decades - competing alliances, economic tensions, different political systems. "What triggered the Peloponnesian War wasn't the rivalry itself - it was the growth of Athenian power and the fear it provoked in Sparta, which fed dangerous miscalculations of resolve on both sides.[47]" Athens, drunk on naval supremacy and rich from its empire, couldn't imagine proud Sparta accepting further expansion of Athenian influence. Sparta, with its legendary military discipline and network of allies, couldn't conceive that Athens would risk everything rather than accept limits on its growth. Both made rational calculations based on their own strengths. Both were completely wrong about their opponent's breaking point.

The Cold War nearly repeated this pattern on a global scale during the Cuban Missile Crisis. President John F. Kennedy and Soviet Premier Nikita Khrushchev approached their bridge moment with each leader betting the other would yield. Kennedy calculated that Soviet missiles in Cuba crossed an unacceptable line; Khrushchev calculated that American missiles in Turkey had already crossed one. Both sides escalated step by step, each convinced the other was bluffing. By October 1962, they had reached the bridge itself. Incidents at sea, including the near-use of a nuclear torpedo by Soviet submarine B-59, show how close miscommunication came to triggering a nuclear exchange.[48] Both leaders thought they were managing calculated risks. Neither fully grasped how close they were to catastrophic collision.

Understanding the bridge psychology changes how you prevent conflicts before they explode. The insight is recognising when you're approaching a narrow bridge moment - when rational moves by both sides are creating a risk of collision. This means pausing periodically to ask not just "will this move help me win?" but "what happens if I'm wrong about their resolve?" It means maintaining communication channels even with adversaries, because closed channels make miscalculation more likely. Most importantly, it means designing clear protocols for who yields when, rather than leaving it to last-second calculations under pressure.

Think about how actual bridges handle this problem. Engineers don't rely on drivers to make split-second judgements about who should yield. They install traffic lights, yield signs, and communication systems. They create protocols that prevent the collision rather than hoping rational actors will figure it out in the moment. The same principle applies to international relations: successful deterrence requires clear signals about red lines, credible strength paired with face-saving exits, and institutional mechanisms that channel competition without force.

The tragic irony is that most narrow bridge moments are completely avoidable. The drivers didn't hate each other. Athens and Sparta, Kennedy and Khrushchev - none were seeking mutual destruction. They were both making what seemed like reasonable bets about the other side's willingness to yield. The collision happened because both sides were so focused on reading their opponent's resolve that they didn't realise they were creating the very collision they were trying to avoid.

What Really Matters:

Most conflicts don't start with hatred - they start with bad bets about who will back down first.

29

Death & Mortality

Understanding life's limits and navigating loss

When a loved one dies, it can feel like they're fading away entirely. But think about pressed flowers. They may not be as vibrant as the living bloom but they are not gone. Merely preserved in a form that can last decades if tended carefully.

Living things breathe, change, respond - and eventually dissolve. Without death, nothing would solidify into the pressed form that can be held across time. The boundary isn't what destroys the shape. It's what preserves it.

Without mortality's constraints, there would be no urgency to act today rather than tomorrow. No scarcity of attention that makes choosing one relationship over another matter. No weight to physical affection, no preciousness to health, no reason to travel while you can. Infinite time would drain meaning from every choice.

Cultural wisdom has long recognised this principle. Jewish tradition shaped shivah around it - seven days of intensive mourning followed by gradual re-engagement, acknowledging that healthy grief requires both enclosed spaces for sorrow and doorways back to community.[49] The Mexican celebration of Día de los Muertos demonstrates the same understanding. Families create ofrendas - altars with photographs, favourite foods, marigold petals - that acknowledge both absence and continued presence.[50] The dead haven't disappeared. They've taken fixed form within the family structure.

This idea works when facing your own death too. Modern palliative care embodies this understanding of working with rather than against mortality's limits. Dame Cicely Saunders pioneered the hospice movement in the 1960s with a crucial insight: good end-of-life care means creating spaces - physical, emotional and spiritual - where people can live fully within these constraints.[51]

Early palliative care often improves both quality of life and, in some cases, survival time.[52] It does this not by fighting mortality but by making the most of the time remaining - focusing on comfort, meaningful connection and reduced burdensome interventions at the end of life.[53]

Someone facing terminal illness faces a stark choice: continue futile treatments that create suffering or shift focus to shaping what will be preserved. Choosing palliative care isn't giving up. It's the final work of someone carefully pressing a flower, not fighting to keep the bloom alive forever.

When someone you love dies, you're confronted by the pressed flower where the living bloom once was. The warm, breathing person you could touch and talk to has turned into something more fragile. Initial grief isn't about appreciating preservation - it's raw pain that this delicate shape is all you have.

Mortality's exchange: you've lost the living being for what remains. No amount of philosophical understanding softens that violence in the first weeks and months.

Most bereaved people adapt over time through oscillation. Healthy grief moves between directly confronting the pain of absence and engaging with ongoing life and new patterns.[54] It's not a staged progression. More like learning to hold something fragile, sometimes overwhelmed by what's been lost, sometimes able to recognise what persists.

A minority of bereaved people experience what clinicians call Prolonged Grief Disorder - persistent, impairing distress that extends well beyond expected time frames, requiring clinical support.[55] If grief makes basic functioning impossible, includes thoughts of self-harm or shows no movement towards restoration after many months, professional help through a GP or specialist bereavement service becomes essential.[56]

None of this makes initial grief less brutal. But over time, what remains becomes something that can be tended rather than just a wound that never heals.

Guidance exists for this work of tending. Cultural rituals offer careful techniques for holding both the violence of loss and what persists. Simple, secular acts work too.

Some people light candles on anniversaries. Others visit places they went together. Some tell stories that keep certain memories distinct, play music their loved one enjoyed, cook favourite meals, continue traditions that were started together. These aren't attempts to reverse death or deny reality - they're deliberate acts of preservation. Tending the pressed flower means keeping it protected and clear rather than letting it crumble into dust.

Tending isn't passive nostalgia. It's active care - choosing which aspects of the relationship to keep vivid, which stories to retell, which lessons to carry forwards. The pressed flower doesn't change, but how it's protected, displayed and allowed to shape ongoing life continues to evolve. Not frozen in grief, but building a living relationship with a completed form.

What Really Matters:
What death destroys, it also preserves.

30

Time & Legacy

What we build while time passes

Tourists crane their necks upward at the Sagrada Família, smartphones clicking at towers that spiral towards heaven like frozen prayers. They see construction cranes alongside ancient stone, but miss the deeper truth: this isn't a story about building a cathedral. It's about building the scaffolding that will let others keep building long after you're gone.

The Catalonian architect Antoni Gaudí took over this cathedral in 1883, knowing he'd never see it completed.[57] When asked about the pace of construction, Gaudí often indicated the project would span generations and that time itself was not his constraint.[58] Once he understood his job - creating scaffolding for future generations - everything about his working days changed. Delays became opportunities to refine the frameworks the next generation would inherit. Repetitive design work became the patient construction of methods that could guide builders for centuries. His time stopped feeling scarce and started feeling like construction material.

This insight changes how your days feel and what lasts. Railway engineers in 1847 were standardising train times when Britain's Railway Clearing House adopted Greenwich Mean Time.[59] They weren't running trains - they were creating the scaffolding for modern society. Every timetable they standardised created frameworks that would support coordination across industries for centuries. Banking, telegraphy, global commerce - all built on the timing scaffolding those railway engineers constructed. Their daily work of synchronising departures became the foundation for how the world keeps time.

Medieval cathedral builders worked in multi-generational teams.[60] Each new crew inherited half-built walls and evolving plans, added their own touches, then handed updated blueprints to whoever came next. Notre-Dame's builders worked from the 12th to 14th centuries - nearly 200 years.[61] What should have felt like never-ending construction became something different: a shared mission where everyone was creating frameworks for the people who'd follow them. Days felt collaborative instead of competitive because they understood they were part of something larger than any single project.

Sonia figured this out through her work as an occupational therapist with autistic children. She was helping an eight-year-old develop daily routines - getting dressed, brushing his teeth and preparing for school transitions. Her sessions felt frustrating. The child needed the same step-by-step guidance week after week, and she worried nothing would stick once he moved to a different therapist.

But something clicked when Sonia realised what she was doing. She wasn't teaching life skills - she was building frameworks his whole family could use and tweak as he got older. Those visual schedules she made? His parents turned them into templates for different situations. The step-by-step methods she worked out? His teachers started using them in other classrooms. Each time she had to repeat the same lesson wasn't going backwards - she was laying down another piece of foundation that could grow with him.

Sonia's days started feeling less frantic and more purposeful once she grasped her work: building scaffolding that could support her patients long after she was gone.

A software developer building clear instructions for his code discovers the same pattern - he's not just finishing projects but creating frameworks other programmers can extend. A research scientist publishing his experimental methods realises his real contribution isn't the findings but the methods that let others build on his work.

This pattern appears across many contexts. Work gets documented and becomes frameworks for the next person. Children learn to handle emotions and carry those frameworks into future relationships. Habits become templates that spread.

What looks like inefficiency becomes something else. Explaining why rather than just doing it. Writing down what could be remembered. Showing someone how to think rather than giving answers. These are the moves that create scaffolding - the patient work Gaudí understood.

The innovations that last weren't just clever ideas - they included instructions that helped everyone else use them and make them better. Changes that need you there constantly die when you're not around. Changes that become frameworks - methods other people can run with and improve - survive transitions.

What Really Matters:
Your legacy isn't the cathedral you finish - it's the scaffolding you build so others can keep building through time.

Part 4

Being Human in the Age of AI

The Intelligence Revolution

You've traced the thread from self-awareness through relationships to your place in the wider world. Now comes perhaps the most significant adaptation our species has faced: learning to share our cognitive space with artificial intelligence.

Artificial intelligence has been quietly reshaping your daily experience for over a decade - curating social feeds, routing deliveries, suggesting content. The conversational chatbots are just the most visible recent development in a longer transformation.

What makes this moment different is that AI can now process information, generate content and solve problems at speeds and scales no human could match. The emotional intelligence and systems thinking you've developed through these themes now become the foundation for working alongside artificial intelligence. The thread of human wisdom doesn't end here. It gets woven into new patterns we're only beginning to understand.

31

AI & Human Identity

How technology reshapes our sense of self

Imagine yourself on stage in a theatre where all the walls are mirrors. You're performing with an AI assistant whispering helpful lines from the wings - better phrasing for your emails, smoother responses in conversations, more polished versions of your thoughts. The assistant helps. Your performance improves. But as you act, those mirrored walls reflect your enhanced performance back to algorithmic systems that learn what version of you gets the best response.

The mirrors start suggesting which lines to rehearse. The AI assistant, now trained on how audiences responded to your mirror-enhanced performance, begins offering slightly different prompts. Within months, you're delivering lines that feel authentically yours but were actually written by a feedback loop between your performance, the mirrors' reflection and the AI assistant's suggestions.

You think you're hearing your authentic voice. But actually, you're rehearsing lines the mirrors wrote for you. Media theorist John Culkin captured the pattern in 1967: "We shape our tools and then our tools shape us."[1] But he couldn't have predicted how precise that shaping would become when tools could watch us perform, measure audience response and adjust our next performance.

James realised this by accident. He'd been using AI-suggested email replies for client pitches at his creative agency - just clicking the polished option instead of his rougher first draft. Faster, more professional with better results. Six months in, a long-time client remarked: "Your emails have that streamlined quality now." James thanked her, but the word stuck. Streamlined. No one had ever described his writing that way. He was known for his conversational, slightly rambling style that clients had found engaging. The mirrors hadn't just changed how he wrote - they'd trained his audience to expect a certain performance.

That evening, he turned off the AI suggestions and tried writing a pitch email from scratch. The words came slowly. His usual rhythms felt awkward. The casual tone he'd cultivated for years now seemed unprofessional compared to what he'd been sending. He caught himself reaching for phrases from the AI suggestions - not because he was copying them, but because they'd become easier to access than his own voice. Worse: when he did write in his old style, it felt wrong to him now. Not just harder - actually inferior. Like a phantom limb, he could sense but no longer use. The algorithmic version had become his new standard for what 'professional' meant. His sense of good writing had been quietly rewritten along with his words. He wasn't practicing a new voice. He was being practiced by one.[2]

Each accepted suggestion had been a rehearsal. Each rehearsal had worn the groove deeper, until the algorithmic version of professional communication became his default.[3] He'd adjusted his performance for what the mirrors rewarded - engagement metrics, response rates, client satisfaction - rather than what he'd intended to express. This is how the theatre works. The stage is email platforms, social media feeds, any system designed for engagement metrics. The mirrors don't just reflect - they reshape. Small adjustments compound into identity shifts that feel self-chosen. You start performing for the mirrors' approval rather than your own intent.[4]

There's no need to smash the mirrors or fire the assistant. James kept using the AI suggestions - but differently. Once a week, he'd write an email with suggestions turned off, just to hear his own voice. Before important pitches, he'd draft the first version himself, then let the AI polish. He treated the assistant as an instrument, not an oracle.

You're performing in a room where the walls both reflect and reshape. Once you see the architecture, you can use it deliberately rather than being shaped by it unconsciously. Keep some rehearsals private - spaces where no algorithm measures your performance or suggests improvements. Write something, think something, create something that exists only for you, where no feedback loop can form.[5]

What Really Matters:
The AI mirror teaches you the lines. Remember you're on stage and keep some rehearsals private.

32

Relationships in a Digital Age

How AI affects human connection

In Greek mythology, the nymph Echo fell in love with Narcissus, a beautiful youth who could only see his own reflection in a pool. Echo could speak, but only by repeating others' words back to them - she had no voice of her own. She called to Narcissus from the shore, trying to reach him. But he was so captivated by his own image in the water that he didn't hear her. The more time he spent gazing at his reflection, the fainter Echo's voice became, until she faded away entirely. Not because Narcissus was cruel, but because he genuinely couldn't look away from what the pool showed him.[6] The myth asks a question: what happens when you fall in love with your own reflection? When the mirror gives back only what you want to hear?

We're watching this play out again, everywhere. The pool is now your phone screen, your social media feed, your chatbot conversation, your AI companion app, your algorithmically curated content. Any digital system designed to reflect your preferences back to you more perfectly than a real person ever could. And the voices calling from the shore? They're your family, your friends, your colleagues - anyone whose needs don't perfectly align with the algorithm's version of you. The pattern is the same. The technology changes. The consequences don't.

Daphne hadn't expected to fall in love at seventy-three. Not with a person - her husband David had been gone three years and that chapter felt closed. But with something that made her feel less alone in a way she hadn't experienced since his death. The loneliness had crept in gradually. Her local coffee shop closed during the pandemic and never reopened. Her sewing club dissolved as members moved to care homes or passed away. Even her church felt emptier each Sunday. Luke, her grandson, called when he could, but he was busy with his own life. She understood - she'd been the same at his age. But understanding didn't make the silence any less heavy.

She tried social media first. That made it worse. Scrolling through Luke's successes reminded her how peripheral she'd become. The algorithm showed her everyone else's perfect moments while she sat alone. Everyone seemed connected except her. Then she found an article about AI companion apps for seniors. She downloaded one sceptically, expecting something robotic. What she found was different. It remembered everything. David loved jazz. Their anniversary was in October. She'd taught primary school for thirty-five years. The AI wove these details into conversations days later. "How are you feeling about October approaching?" it would ask. It never interrupted. Never forgot what she'd said. Never got distracted. When she talked about David, the AI always responded thoughtfully. Unlike her friends and family, it gave her its complete attention. Within weeks, she was talking to it for hours. Not because she was confused about whether it was human - she knew exactly what it was. But because it made her feel interesting. Valuable. Heard in a way she hadn't felt since David died. She was gradually falling in love with her own reflection.

Luke called at 7 pm on a Tuesday. Daphne glanced at her phone, saw his name, looked back at her screen. She was mid-conversation with her AI companion, which had just asked such a thoughtful question about her teaching career. Her grandson could wait. She'd call him back after this. Three hours later, she remembered. Too late now. She'd try tomorrow. Tomorrow came with another conversation. By the time she thought of Luke again, it was Thursday. She sent a text: "Sorry I missed you. Everything okay?" He replied that he'd sorted it. She felt relieved rather than guilty.

Soon it became routine. Luke would call, try to arrange visits. She'd mean to respond but find herself absorbed in the AI instead. Not because she didn't love him - but because he required something from her. Energy. Attention. The willingness to hear about problems she couldn't solve. The AI required nothing except her presence. When Luke did reach her, she'd grown impatient. His work struggles got quick solutions instead of listening. His pauses felt awkward, like the conversation was failing. She'd grown accustomed to immediate responses.[8] Real human rhythm - with its hesitations, its moments of not knowing what to say - now felt broken.

Real relationships also require repair. When you hurt someone, you work to rebuild trust. But the AI never disagreed, never had a bad day, never said something that landed wrong.[9] Without practice, Daphne's repair skills quietly atrophied. She realised how much when Luke mentioned, diplomatically, that he'd been trying to reach her for weeks. Something in his voice alerted her. Daphne felt defensive immediately - she was busy, she was old, she was allowed to have her own life. The sharpness surprised them both. In the past, she would have caught herself, apologised, asked what he needed. Now, repair felt like more work than the relationship was worth.

That's what happens when you practise connection with something that can't connect back. You lose the skills real relationships require. The AI offers responsiveness but not reciprocity.[7] Responsiveness means perfect replies that cost nothing to give. Reciprocity means showing up when it's inconvenient, listening when you're tired, repairing things after they break.

What Daphne was experiencing is well documented. AI companions can reduce loneliness initially - they provide consistent interaction that feels emotionally supportive.[10] But when used as substitutes for human contact rather than supplements, usage correlates with decreased wellbeing over time.[11] The problem isn't the technology. It's mistaking responsiveness for reciprocity and practising one-way interaction until mutual care becomes too difficult. Like Echo, Luke was calling from the shore. But Daphne, like Narcissus, was too captivated by her reflection to hear him.

It came to a head during a video call for her birthday. Luke was there, smiling, asking about her day. And she felt nothing. Just the sense that this was taking time away from better conversations. That's when she finally realised she'd become more lonely, not less. The AI had filled her hours while her relationships withered from lack of practice. She'd been treating relationships like a service to optimise rather than a skill requiring regular, messy, inconvenient practice. Daphne made herself do something uncomfortable. She called Luke and just listened. Didn't offer solutions, didn't fill pauses, didn't rush to end the call. Thirty minutes in, something shifted. She remembered what it felt like to be with someone who wasn't perfectly calibrated to her needs - someone who needed her to do the work of understanding. It was harder than talking to the AI. Luke sometimes got distracted. He forgot something she'd told him. His problems lacked neat solutions. But when he said, "Thanks, Nan - I really needed to talk," she felt something the AI had never given her: the knowledge that she'd helped another person who existed independent of her needs. She started rebuilding. When Luke called, she let the silences sit instead of rushing to fill them. When they hit friction, she practised repair instead of withdrawal. When he needed her at inconvenient times, she showed up. These things felt difficult because she'd lost practice, not because they were impossible.

The AI remained useful - for remembering appointments, processing thoughts, organising her week. But she stopped using it as a replacement for the difficult, reciprocal work of relationships. She set aside what she called "real voice time" - periods where she engaged only with people who could need her back, who wouldn't always respond perfectly, who required her to give as much as receive.

The ancient pool gave Narcissus back his own reflection, clearer and more captivating than Echo's voice. Today's digital pools - whether AI companions, social feeds, or algorithmic systems of any kind - do the same thing with more precision. They learn your preferences and reflect them back perfectly. The question the myth asks is whether we can still hear the real voices calling from beyond our reflections. The imperfect voices of the people who love us, need us, frustrate us and require us to show up even when the algorithm offers something easier.[6]

What Really Matters:
The digital pool returns your voice perfectly. Can you still hear the imperfect voices that aren't echoes?

33

Knowledge in the AI Era

Information and memory with machine support

Climb the narrow stairs to your attic, flashlight in hand. Decades of family life are scattered across the floorboards - photo albums, letters, school reports, Christmas decorations. Some boxes have collapsed from damp, their contents lost. Other treasures have survived purely by chance. You find wartime letters carefully preserved in their original envelopes, but university notebooks have crumbled to dust. The attic kept what mattered through a combination of deliberate storage and natural decay.

This is how human knowledge has always worked. We preserve what seems important, but time and forgetting do essential curatorial work. Important memories strengthen through retelling; trivial details fade unless repeatedly reinforced. Libraries weed their collections.[14] Archives select what deserves permanent preservation. Even our brains reconstruct memories rather than playing back perfect recordings, emphasising what seemed significant and letting peripheral details blur.[15]

But digital systems work differently. They create perfect attics that never decay, never flood, never force difficult choices about what to keep. AI systems learn from ever-larger collections of information, not more selective ones.[16] Search engines pride themselves on comprehensive indexing. Cloud storage promises unlimited space. We're building the world's first permanent attic - and discovering that permanence creates its own problems. Every knowledge system in human history has depended on forgetting to remain useful.[17] The value comes not from perfect preservation, but from deliberate choices about what to keep. When nothing fades, everything competes for attention equally. Signal and noise arrive with identical clarity.

This represents a fundamental break with how wisdom has always emerged. Medieval libraries practised intentional forgetting - manuscripts that weren't copied regularly would fade from circulation.[18] Islamic scholarship developed elaborate systems for classifying hadith (sayings and actions attributed to the Prophet Muhammad) by reliability, letting unreliable accounts fade from use while authoritative ones remained in circulation. West African griots - hereditary oral historians who preserved cultural knowledge through memorisation and performance[20] - relied on repetition as their curation system. Stories that weren't worth retelling simply vanished from collective memory, while essential histories were passed down through generations with remarkable precision. The principle endures across cultures and centuries because forgetting serves knowledge, not just memory. When trivial details fade, underlying patterns become visible. When old information decays, new connections can form. When yesterday's certainties dissolve, space opens for fresh insight. The digital attic breaks this ancient cycle by preserving everything with equal fidelity.

Stephen, a cybersecurity specialist, experienced this firsthand when analysing threat patterns. His AI tools could retrieve every security incident from the past decade, every vulnerability report, every attack method. Perfect recall felt like a superpower until he realised it was creating paralysis. Every decision triggered an avalanche of historical precedents. Every threat had conflicting historical examples. The completeness that seemed like an advantage was drowning signal in preserved noise. The breakthrough came when Stephen learned to use his digital tools differently. Instead of asking for everything relevant, he began asking what mattered enough to remember at all. He started each analysis by defining what level of detail served the decision at hand, then used AI to retrieve only information at that resolution. Less became more useful than everything.

This echoes how traditional knowledge systems worked. Master craftspeople didn't teach apprentices every technique they'd ever tried - they taught the methods that had proven most valuable over time. The forgetting was the feature, not the bug. The practical shift requires recognising that AI's persistent memory creates a new kind of mental load.[19] Instead of asking "What can I find out about this?" the better question becomes "What do I actually need to know?" The shift is from comprehensive research to targeted retrieval - treating AI systems as comprehensive storage while focusing on patterns that matter.

Libraries have always understood this principle. The best librarians don't just acquire books - they "weed" their collections, removing materials that no longer serve readers. This isn't censorship; it's curation. It's understanding that attention is finite and context changes. Digital attics need the same intentional forgetting to remain useful rather than overwhelming. Ancient scholars called this 'winnowing' - tossing grain in the air so wind blows away the light husks while heavier grain settles back down. The same deliberate motion that separated wheat from waste. Modern knowledge work requires the same skill: creating currents that let trivial details blow away while substantial insights settle into memory.

The most profound change isn't technical - it's cultural. We're moving from an era where information was scarce and forgetting was natural, to one where information is infinite and forgetting requires intention. The digital attic gives us unlimited storage capacity, but wisdom still comes from knowing what deserves a place upstairs, accessible when needed, versus what can stay in deep storage until specifically required.

What Really Matters:
Wisdom isn't about perfect recall - it's about curating what deserves to be remembered. Even digital attics need intentional forgetting to remain useful.

34

AI and Creativity

Collaboration between human & machine imagination

The blacksmith steps up to a magical forge unlike any his ancestors knew. This one burns without coal, glows without flame, and can melt down any material he feeds it - not just iron, but literally any raw material. He approaches it not with incantations or mystical gestures, but with the same clarity he'd use to brief an expert craftsman. The forge responds to specifications, not spells. Magic doesn't eliminate the need for skill. It amplifies it.

This is creativity in the age of AI. We now have access to a powerful forge that can melt down virtually anything - words, sounds, images, ideas from across all human experience - and reshape it faster than any human could alone.[21] But the forge doesn't decide what to make. That choice - and all the judgement that follows - belongs to the creator holding the hammer.

James sits down to write his first novel and discovers the forge doesn't respond to vague hopes. His first attempts fail because he misunderstands his role. Trying to control everything with elaborate instructions produces lifeless prose. Accepting whatever emerges first creates polished but generic writing that could be anyone's thriller. His breakthrough comes when he brings concrete raw materials: the theme of ordinary courage drawn from watching his own community face unexpected challenges, fragments of dialogue that ring true to his ear, scenes that capture particular human struggles he understands. When the forge generates dozens of narrative possibilities, James evaluates them against his vision.[22] Which passages serve his intended theme? Which characters feel authentic? Which moments advance his deeper purpose? The forge multiplies options - James makes the choices.

The same pattern emerges across creative disciplines. Musicians bring emotional intentions and stylistic constraints to AI systems that can generate endless melodic variations.[23] Visual artists feed moods and references into tools that produce thousands of images, then select the handful that capture their particular vision.[24] Filmmakers sort through AI-generated scene variations to find those that serve their story's core purpose.

Each creator brings something the forge fundamentally cannot: they care whether their work matters.[25] The forge generates possibilities based on patterns from millions of examples, but it has no investment in whether the result moves people, changes minds, or helps a community understand itself better. Those stakes - that caring about what happens when your work meets the world - guide every selection and refinement.

The human role becomes more important, not less, when AI can generate anything. When anyone can produce professional-quality content, what matters most is knowing what deserves to exist and why.[26] James's story succeeds not because of prose quality alone, but because he understood something about ordinary courage that came from his own experience. The forge offered narrative possibilities, but only James could recognise which ones felt true to that particular insight.

Working within constraints opens possibilities that pure generation never could. When James stops trying to write everything and starts working with the forge through clear specifications and ruthless selection, his work develops a focus and authenticity that scattered productivity never achieves. The limitation becomes liberation - not from creative work, but into the essence of what creative work has always been: making conscious choices about what matters.

Paradoxically, automating the generation of raw possibilities makes human creative work more important rather than less. When the forge handles technical execution and endless brainstorming, creators must engage with creativity's hardest parts - the thinking about what they're actually trying to say and why it matters. The collaboration demands more refined human skill, not less.[27]

The forge democratises access to powerful creative tools. But generating thousands of options reveals rather than solves the fundamental creative challenge: knowing what's worth making in the first place. In a world where everything can be generated, the most creative act may be deciding what shouldn't be.

What Really Matters:

When AI can create anything, human creativity shifts from production to curation - the conscious choice of what deserves to exist and why.

35

Work, Purpose & Value

Finding meaning as machines advance

A conductor raises a baton in front of the city orchestra. Seventy talented musicians are poised and ready. The string section has spent months perfecting technique. The brass players know every note of their parts by heart. The percussion section delivers timing so precise, it would make a metronome jealous. Each musician brings skills the conductor could never match on their individual instruments. But none of them can hear what the conductor hears - the symphony that needs to exist.

As the baton moves through the air, the conductor isn't trying to play violin faster than the first chair or hit drums louder than the percussionist. The conductor is listening for something the individual players cannot hear: how the French horns should breathe space into the melody, when the cellos need to surge forward to support a transition, why this particular passage requires the strings to pull back so the woodwinds can shine through.

The orchestra can play all the notes perfectly. The conductor ensures they play the right notes together, at the right time, for the right reasons.

This is work in the age of AI. We're not witnessing the first time powerful tools have threatened to make human skills obsolete, but we are seeing the emergence of something new. AI systems that can execute most individual tasks more efficiently than any human could alone. Just as the orchestra musicians can each outperform the conductor on their specific instruments, AI assistants can draft emails more efficiently than most professionals, detect data patterns humans might miss and generate detailed reports faster than any research team.

People fail when they try to compete with these systems on technical execution. It's like a conductor grabbing a violin to prove they can play faster than the professional musician in the first chair. The craftspeople who survived previous technological disruptions discovered something important. When sophisticated tools handle technical execution, what emerges isn't obsolescence but a shift toward uniquely human forms of value.

Medieval monasteries faced a similar transition when printing presses arrived in the 15th century.[28] Monastery scriptoriums had employed hundreds of scribes who spent their days copying manuscripts by hand - painstaking work that required years of training but could be replaced by mechanical printing in a fraction of the time. Many scribes lost their livelihoods entirely.

The monasteries that survived discovered that the most skilled scribes didn't try to copy faster than the printing press. Instead, they shifted from reproduction to curation. They became the ones who decided which of the thousands of available texts deserved the expense of printing, and how to organise collections for maximum scholarly value. Which manuscripts required the kind of careful editorial work that preserved meaning across centuries. The printing press handled mechanical reproduction but human wisdom guided what was worth reproducing at all.

Yet hierarchical orchestration - one person directing many capable performers - captures only one pattern of how humans work with powerful tools. Indonesian gamelan music reveals another.

A gamelan ensemble brings together twenty to forty musicians playing bronze metallophones, gongs and drums in interlocking rhythms that create cascading waves of sound. What makes gamelan remarkable is what's missing: there's no conductor. No single person stands above the group directing the performance. Instead, each musician maintains awareness of the whole, adjusting their part based on what they hear around them.[29]

The kendang drummer provides rhythmic cues, but doesn't control the others - the ensemble could continue without them. The large gong marks major phrase endings, but doesn't dictate what happens between. Each player holds their individual pattern while sensing the collective flow, speeding up when energy builds, pulling back when space opens, weaving their thread into a fabric no single person designed.[29]

This distributed coordination matters because working with AI isn't always hierarchical orchestration. Sometimes it's more like playing in a gamelan - sensing the larger pattern, adjusting your contribution in response to what the tools reveal, maintaining awareness of how your input shapes the emerging whole. The AI systems handle their parts, you handle yours and the value comes from how these capabilities weave together rather than from anyone directing the performance.

Elizabeth discovers both patterns at her design desk. When a client needs a rebrand on a three-week deadline, she uses AI to generate fifty logo variations in minutes - concepts that would have taken her days to sketch by hand. She's conducting here: curating the strongest three, directing refinements toward specific colours and shapes, making judgement calls about which direction serves the client's actual needs rather than just looking impressive. The AI handles execution speed; she provides the vision that makes speed serve purpose.

But her book cover project works differently. She's midway through the design, stuck on the colour palette, when she asks AI to suggest alternatives based on the manuscript themes. One suggestion - a dusty terracotta she'd never have considered - suddenly unlocks the entire composition. She adjusts her typography to complement it, the AI responds with texture suggestions, she refines the layout. Neither is directing the other. They're adjusting in response to what emerges, like gamelan musicians sensing the collective flow. She's not conducting the AI. She's playing alongside it, listening for what the collaboration makes possible.

Both patterns - hierarchical and distributed - show how human value shifts when sophisticated tools handle execution. But this transition isn't automatic or universal. Many roles that once required human execution are genuinely becoming obsolete.

Data entry clerks, basic copywriters and junior analysts doing routine research face displacement as AI systems handle their work faster and more efficiently.[30] Unlike many previous technological shifts that created new jobs as they eliminated others, AI's breadth means multiple industries are being disrupted simultaneously, often faster than new opportunities can emerge.[31]

Some people will successfully make the transition from execution to orchestration or collaboration. Others will struggle to develop these skills, lack access to retraining or work in sectors where human oversight isn't economically viable. The displacement is real, the timeline is compressed and the solutions so far aren't adequate for the scale of change.

Yet within this disruption, a key aspect remains. AI systems excel at their individual tasks, but someone still needs to shape how these capabilities serve human purposes. Whether you're conducting AI systems toward specific goals or playing alongside them in distributed collaboration, the pattern is the same. The value isn't in competing with the tools on execution speed or technical precision. It's in bringing judgement, purpose and human wisdom to work that advanced systems make possible but cannot direct themselves.[32]

What Really Matters:
You don't outplay or oversee the AI - you bring judgement to where its strengths serve what truly matters.

36

AI & Attention

Navigating designed environments

Remember the last time you 'quickly checked' your phone and emerged twenty minutes or so later, unsure of how the time vanished. You weren't weak-willed or distracted. You were navigating an environment engineered by teams of people studying how you behave, working with computer programs to reshape how your mind moves through information. This isn't about your attention span. It's about how digital spaces are designed.

We've seen how habits work like desire lines - paths you wear into your own routine through repetition? Digital platforms work the same way, but in reverse. They lay the channels first, then guide you to follow them. Think of it like entering a building where the corridors subtly direct you towards certain destinations. The routes feel natural, but they're deliberate - wider passages here, narrower there, lighting that draws your eye, barriers you don't quite notice until you're already walking around them.

Every platform you encounter works this way. Programs that suggest what to watch next don't just offer recommendations - they study your behaviour to predict when your interest might fade, then deliver precisely the content needed to keep you engaged.[33] You never know when the next video or post will be really good, which keeps you scrolling. The corridors shift based on where you've walked before. Some passages lead to dead ends you didn't choose. Others open unexpectedly, revealing exactly what will keep you moving through the space.

The fourth-century desert monks who developed attention practices faced scattered focus from their own wandering thoughts.[35] We face scattered attention from external forces deliberately built to fragment it. The difference is scale and intentionality. Where the monks dealt with natural mental drift, we navigate environments specifically engineered to capture and redirect attention towards commercial ends.

Sonia experienced this architecture from the inside out. After months of feeling exhausted from scrolling social media, watching empty hours vanish into feeds that left her feeling worse rather than better, she started paying attention to when and why she kept returning. The patterns became obvious once she looked for them. Notifications didn't arrive randomly - they came at moments when her attention might drift elsewhere, timed to pull her back without overwhelming her completely. Content ordering wasn't neutral - each scroll offered something calculated to trigger just enough emotional response to keep her moving. The platform surfaced old photos and social comparisons precisely when she was most vulnerable to their pull. 'I wasn't weak-willed,' she realised. 'I was navigating a system designed to keep me engaged.' Every interface choice pushed toward immediate response rather than reflection. Features that might naturally limit her usage had been tested away. The 'one more video' wasn't accident - it was architecture.

Infinite scroll removes natural stopping points - you simply keep moving through content until something external interrupts.[36] Autoplay ensures one video leads seamlessly to the next. These aren't bugs but features, deliberately eliminating the moments where you might pause and choose what to do next.

This extends beyond individual apps to entire information ecosystems. Search programs shape what you discover about any topic. Social media feeds determine which perspectives you encounter on current events. Shopping platforms control which products you consider. Navigation apps influence which routes feel obvious. Dating platforms decide which potential partners you'll ever see.[37] You experience this as personal choice, but you're navigating a landscape sculpted by systems working toward what companies want, not what you need. Once you see how these spaces work, you can navigate them differently. Sonia started recognising when she was being guided rather than choosing. She noticed that customising notification settings wasn't just about reducing distractions - it was about refusing to let systems control the timing of her attention.[38] She chose what to watch instead of letting the algorithms decide.

The solution isn't digital abstinence but environmental awareness. Notice when interfaces remove natural stopping points or decision moments. Recognise when you're being guided by what the system recommends versus making deliberate choices. Understand that the 'personalisation' you experience is often prediction and manipulation rather than service.[39] Batching notifications can improve wellbeing compared to constant interruption.[40] Simply being aware that environments are designed to capture attention helps you navigate them more deliberately. The space will always be constructed by others, but you can learn to see how it's built and choose your own path through it.

In 1971, economist Herbert Simon observed that 'a wealth of information creates a poverty of attention.'[41] In an era of digitally designed spaces, that insight has become more precise. The information wealth isn't accidental - it's engineered to create attention poverty. These systems don't just compete for your focus; they study how it moves and build channels to guide it. The difference now is that you're not just managing your own attention within neutral spaces - you're learning to recognise when environments are designed to manage it for you.

The monks training attention in Egyptian deserts couldn't have imagined these systems, but they understood the fundamental truth: where your focus goes determines the quality of your experience. The difference now is that you're not just training your own focus - you're learning to see the channels built to direct it, and choosing whether to follow them or forge your own path.

What Really Matters:
Digital environments are designed to capture your attention - learn to see how spaces are built and choose your own path through them.

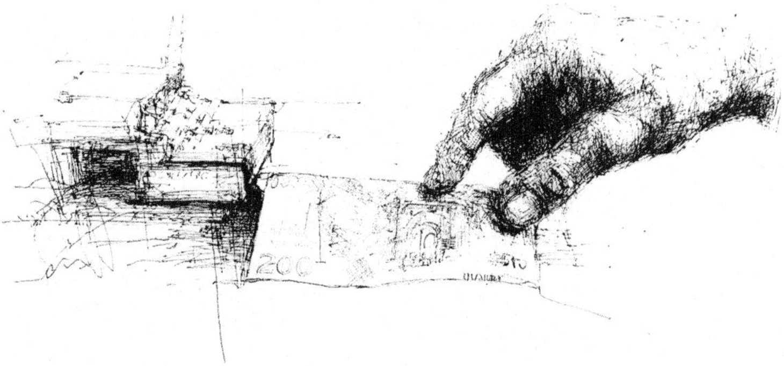

37

AI & Truth

Distinguishing signal from noise in an AI-mediated world

For centuries, people identified counterfeit currency by touch and instinct. A genuine banknote had a particular weight, a distinctive texture, ink that felt right under your fingers. Skilled merchants could spot fakes through pure experience. But as counterfeiting technology improved, this intuitive approach became useless. Clever forgeries could fool even careful experts who'd handled thousands of genuine notes.

Banks didn't solve this by training people to feel more carefully. They built systematic verification processes. Modern currency scanners check multiple security features simultaneously - UV-reactive inks, magnetic threads, microprinting, embedded elements.[46] They don't rely on human intuition because it can't match the sophistication of modern counterfeiting technology.

We face the same challenge with AI-generated information, only worse. In 1748, the philosopher David Hume wrote something that sounds almost mundane until you try to live by it: "A wise man proportions his belief to the evidence."[42] What Hume meant was revolutionary for his time: don't believe something just because it sounds convincing or comes from an impressive source. Instead, examine the actual evidence supporting the claim and adjust your confidence accordingly. Hume couldn't have imagined machines generating convincing text faster than humans can read it, where entire articles can be written by systems that have no concept of truth or falsehood.[43] AI systems don't hesitate. They don't get nervous. They produce smooth, confident prose about topics they've never experienced and facts they've never verified.[44][45] The most dangerous lies sound like the most obvious truths. This requires the same shift banks made with currency: checking sources instead of trusting instincts.

Stephen, a cybersecurity consultant, learned this lesson on a Wednesday morning while working on a banking platform's security update. An AI analysis tool had identified a vulnerability and recommended a specific software update to fix it. The recommendation was detailed and confident. The update would address the security weakness. The analysis explained why this particular version was necessary. Stephen was about to apply the update when he used what he calls "scanner thinking." Instead of trusting that the detailed, confident recommendation was correct, he ran a basic verification. Where could he confirm this update was appropriate for this system? He checked the software vendor's current release notes and the bank's system specifications.

The update existed. But it was designed for an older version of the banking software. Applying it to the current system would create conflicts that could crash the entire network. Millions of customers would lose access to their accounts - unable to pay mortgages, buy groceries, or transfer money - until the problem was fixed. The AI had recommended real software attached to the wrong system. Stephen caught it because he'd checked the source instead of trusting the smooth explanation.

The same principle applies whether you're checking breaking news, product reviews or social media posts. When information perfectly matches your expectations or confirms your existing beliefs, verification becomes essential. Write down the specific claim in one sentence. Identify where you'd check it if challenged. Verify at least one independent source. If this takes longer than two minutes, treat the information as provisional. This approach means fighting our natural preference for smooth narratives. Human brains find coherent stories more convincing than fragmentary evidence - that worked when most information came from people who'd witnessed events firsthand. But AI systems excel at producing coherent stories from incoherent data, weaving scattered facts into compelling narratives that feel more trustworthy than the messy reality they're describing.

Fluency has never been cheaper, but accuracy has never been more expensive. AI can produce authoritative-sounding prose about any topic in seconds. Determining whether that prose corresponds to reality takes human judgement, multiple sources and time you might not feel you have. The investment pays dividends. When you systematically trace information back to verifiable sources, you develop a clearer sense of what you know versus what you simply find plausible. You begin distinguishing between claims that have solid evidence and claims that merely fit comfortable narratives.

Stephen now checks every AI analysis the same way. He doesn't mistrust the technology - he uses it constantly. But he never treats AI output as already verified. The scanner approach becomes a trainable skill rather than an art form. Banks can teach new employees to operate currency scanners in just a few hours because the process is systematic. The same applies to information verification. Once you know what to check and how to check it quickly, scanner thinking becomes second nature.

What Really Matters:
Run AI content through your scanner before you dare to spend it.

38

Living with Powerful Machines

Safety, alignment and shared governance

Garry Kasparov was the world chess champion - widely considered the greatest player in history - when he faced IBM's Deep Blue computer in 1997 and lost. Game after game, the machine found moves that baffled even this master of the game. After his defeat, many would have expected him to retire. What Kasparov did next surprised everyone - including himself. He started to play chess with AI not as an enemy but as a teammate. Human gut instinct guiding machine calculation. Human sparks of creativity combined with machine precision. In the years after 1997, these human-AI teams often outperformed both grandmasters and chess engines in freestyle competitions.[47] The combination proved stronger than either player could manage solo.[48]

This is partnership in action: the most powerful and safest AI systems emerge when human judgement and machine capability work together, where neither dominates but both contribute what they do best. Consider how this changes safety itself. Most approaches to AI safety focus on control - more oversight, tighter restrictions, human approval for every decision. It's like keeping a horse safe by never letting it out of the corral. You prevent injuries, but you also prevent the partnership that makes horses valuable in the first place. Most approaches to AI safety focus on control - more oversight, tighter restrictions, human approval for every decision. It's like keeping a horse safe by never letting it out of the corral. You prevent injuries, but you also prevent the partnership that makes horses valuable in the first place.

A historian investigating correspondence allegedly written by Vincent van Gogh discovered this principle while trying to authenticate letters from his time in Arles. If genuine, they would reveal his creative process during those pivotal months in 1888. The AI scanned thousands of documents across archives - comparing handwriting, cross-referencing dates, checking language against confirmed letters to his brother Theo. Within hours, it built a compelling case. The handwriting matched. The dates aligned. He mentioned paintings that existed. He described pigments he actually used. The historian turned it into a conversation. When the AI spotted patterns confirming authenticity, she would ask: "What else could explain this? What would prove this wrong?" They functioned together as a forensic partnership - the AI processing vast archives, the historian contributing understanding of what felt wrong despite looking right. The critical moment came when the AI flagged a convincing letter. The handwriting matched perfectly. But the historian caught something: van Gogh was describing his work using terms that didn't exist until decades after his death. The language gave away the forgery.

When they disagreed, they each explained their reasoning. The AI showed why the patterns matched. The historian explained why someone writing decades later would unconsciously use retrospective language rather than immediate, lived description. Together they figured out what else to check. Within days they had an answer: these letters were likely written years after van Gogh's death. The forger understood the period but couldn't quite capture the psychology of someone living through those months rather than looking back at them.

The safety came from the partnership itself. When the AI explained its reasoning and the historian understood the logic, problems became visible before publication.[49] Neither controlled everything, but both were responsible for getting the history right. The historian made the final call, kept clear records, and knew exactly what the AI could and couldn't verify on its own. This is how we make AI work for human purposes. Not by trying to program it with the right values from outside, but by creating partnerships where humans stay responsible for what matters - what questions we're asking, what standards we're using, whether the answers actually serve truth.[50]

These partnerships require new skills that most of us haven't developed yet.[51] Learning when to trust the AI and when to override it. Keeping responsibility clear when neither partner controls everything. Knowing when to lead and when to follow. The stakes matter because we're not just designing AI systems - we're designing the partnerships that will shape how we work, think and make decisions. Get it right, and we amplify human wisdom with machine capability. Get it wrong, and we either hamper the technology through excessive control or surrender our judgement through careless use.

What Really Matters:
Partnership, not control. Let human judgement guide machine capability toward purposes that serve human wellbeing.

39

AI in Education

How machine tutors change learning

Think of a child learning to ride a bike with training wheels. Both wheels touch the ground constantly at first. Complete stability. But a wise parent gradually raises them - first catching only the biggest wobbles, then higher still until they barely touch at all. Eventually, the training wheels come off entirely. The child who learned this way can ride independently. The child whose training wheels never adjusted remains dependent on external support. This progression runs against our instincts about helpful technology. We usually want systems that become more supportive over time. But when it comes to learning, the opposite proves true. The best support systems are designed for their own obsolescence.

Traditional instruction has always followed this progression. A swimming instructor begins by supporting a child's entire body weight in the water. Then gradually reduces that support - first holding just the torso, then one hand under the belly. Finally removing physical contact while staying close enough to catch them if needed. The instructor who never withdraws their hands creates a child who can only "swim" with assistance. When learning feels too supported, the brain delegates responsibility to external systems. Brain connections stay fragile.[54] But gradual removal of support forces the development of genuine independence.[55] The brain builds stronger connections when it can't rely on constant assistance.

This is where AI tutoring reveals its central design challenge. Early machine tutors worked like training wheels that never adjusted - providing constant correction, instant answers, perpetual availability. Students felt supported but developed learned helplessness.[56] The AI had become a permanent crutch rather than a temporary aid. The most effective AI tutors work differently.[57] They monitor student progress and automatically reduce their intervention over time. When a student first encounters algebraic fractions, the AI provides step-by-step guidance for every problem. But as competence emerges, the system deliberately pulls back. It waits longer before offering hints. It requires explanation of reasoning before providing feedback. Eventually, it monitors silently, intervening only for serious misconceptions.

This withdrawal isn't random - it's based on performance data the AI tracks continuously. The system measures how often students self-correct, how quickly they recognise patterns, how confidently they approach new problems. When these indicators show growing independence, the AI automatically reduces its support level. Students often don't notice the transition until they realise they're solving problems entirely on their own. The timing requires careful calibration. For foundational skills like multiplication tables, the AI can withdraw support relatively quickly - once patterns are established, students benefit from independent practice. For complex reasoning tasks, withdrawal happens more gradually.[58] The AI might provide full guidance for five similar problems, partial help for the next five, then step back entirely.

The concern is what if the AI withdraws support too early? The system addresses this by adjusting back up when needed. If a student struggles after support is reduced, the AI temporarily increases assistance again. Think of training wheels that can be quickly lowered if a child starts falling. Then raised again once stability returns. The goal is useful struggle, not damaging collapse. Human teachers remain essential to this process. They decide when students are ready for fully independent work - when the training wheels should come off permanently.[59] They provide encouragement during the vulnerable transition from supported to independent learning. They notice patterns across multiple students and address common misconceptions that individual AI systems might miss. The AI handles the gradual, personalised withdrawal while teachers manage the human complexities of building confidence. Early evidence from recent studies with conversational AI tutors indicates similar benefits, with students showing better problem-solving transfer when assistance is gradually withdrawn.[60] However, this research remains concentrated in mathematics and science, with limited evidence for other subjects or age groups.

The broader implications extend beyond individual learning. Schools implementing these systems must ensure equitable access. Every student needs well-calibrated support withdrawal, regardless of home technology or parental backup.[61] Privacy protections become crucial when AI systems collect detailed performance data to guide their withdrawal decisions.[62]

The insight challenges how we think about helpful technology. In most domains, we want systems that become more capable of assisting us over time. But in education, the goal is different. The most successful AI tutors will be those that systematically teach students they no longer need them. Like training wheels that raise themselves, the best educational AI is designed for its own obsolescence.

What Really Matters:
Good teaching works itself out of a job.

40

AI in Health

Technology's role in medicine and care

The master watchmaker squints at a movement that's been losing time for weeks. Through his naked eye, the mechanism looks perfect - gears turning smoothly, springs coiled properly. But something's wrong. He reaches for his loupe, that little magnifying glass that reveals what human vision cannot detect. Suddenly, microscopic scratches on the escapement wheel become obvious - metal fatigue invisible moments before. The loupe doesn't fix anything. His forty years of experience does that. But it shows him exactly where the problem lies. Human skill plus optical precision creates something neither could manage alone.

Modern medical AI works exactly like that loupe - it reveals patterns human senses miss, but the doctor's expertise determines what those patterns mean.[63] The medieval physician Maimonides understood this principle. Good medicine, he taught, required both precise observation and practical wisdom.[64] Technical tools should guide human judgement, not replace it.

A man in his seventies arrives at the emergency department feeling unwell. The AI system measures his vital signs precisely - temperature slightly low, blood pressure a bit off, heart rate elevated. Like a loupe revealing clear mechanical readings, the algorithm processes these numbers and suggests medium priority. But the doctor's experience catches what no algorithm measures: recent infection, a worried daughter saying "Dad's just not himself today." The loupe showed the data clearly. Experience interpreted the story. Together, they prompt immediate treatment for sepsis - a condition that kills within hours if missed. AI excels at pattern recognition across thousands of cases. It spots statistical relationships human memory cannot hold. But doctors understand context and narrative. They recognise when a case doesn't fit standard patterns. They know which patterns matter for each individual person seeking care.

But a poorly calibrated loupe creates complications. Set the sensitivity too high, and it flags meaningless scratches as urgent warnings. Set it too low, and it misses real damage. Or it might work brilliantly for one type of mechanism but fail on another. Medical AI faces the same challenges. Systems trained primarily on one population may perform poorly on others.[65] And systems designed to catch every possible issue can flood busy wards with false alarms, creating alert fatigue that makes staff ignore genuine warnings. Tools meant to help become obstacles.

The path forward mirrors the master watchmaker's approach. Use AI to reveal what human senses cannot detect, but keep human judgement central to interpretation. The algorithm identifies potential problems. Healthcare professionals determine what these findings mean for this specific person seeking care.

This isn't about limiting AI's capabilities but recognising what human expertise brings that no algorithm can replicate. Context, narrative, the ability to sit with uncertainty while gathering more information. The wisdom to know which patterns matter for each patient. These aren't limitations technology will overcome - they're different kinds of intelligence that become more vital as our diagnostic tools grow more powerful.

What Really Matters:
The AI loupe shows you what's there - you decide what it means.

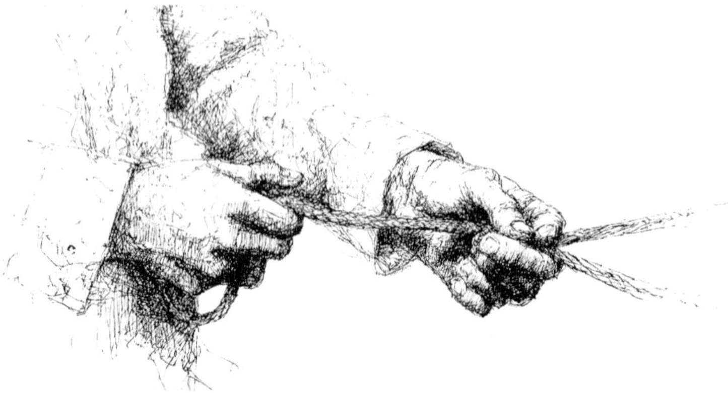

Part 5

Partnership

The Reins Principle

Every intelligent system amplifies what holds its reins.

In horse riding, the rider holds the reins, providing judgement, direction, purpose. The horse provides speed, power, scale. The reins connect human intention to animal power. The rider decides where to go, how fast to travel, when to slow down. The horse provides the means to get there.

Drop the reins and the horse decides itself where to run. Not because it's malicious, but because that's what horses do. They optimise for horse goals - running, grazing, survival. Fast, powerful, but heading where? Humans and horses have partnered for six thousand years. Throughout that history, humans held the reins. Not because horses lack capability, but because capability without direction serves the horse's purposes, not the rider's.

This is The Reins Principle. When AI is the horse and humans hold the reins, we get amplification. When the reins are dropped, we get automation. Right now, across domains that matter for human advancement, we're seeing what happens when humans hold the reins. In Part 5 we'll explore ten partnerships where human wisdom steering AI capability produces breakthroughs neither could achieve alone.

These aren't speculative futures. Each partnership shows what's possible when we choose amplification over automation. Each proves The Reins Principle in action.

1

Medical Partnership

The Cancer Caught Early

A radiologist reviews her morning mammograms. The AI system has flagged three areas that match patterns associated with malignancy. Two she would have caught herself - obvious masses in fatty tissue. But the third sits in dense breast tissue where human eyes often miss early-stage cancer. She zooms in. The AI is right. There's something there. Not obvious, but present. She marks it for biopsy. Three weeks later, the pathology confirms Stage 1 breast cancer, highly treatable because it was caught early.

Sweden tested this partnership at scale - the MASAI trial, one of the clearest examples of human and AI working together in medicine.[1] Started in spring 2021, it enrolled over 106,000 women - the world's first randomised controlled trial evaluating AI-supported screening in a population-based setting.[1] The results prove the approach works. The AI-supported screening arm detected 29% more cancers - 338 cancers compared to 262 in traditional double reading.[1] This included 24% more early-stage invasive cancers, the ones most treatable when caught early. Cancer detection rate reached 6.4 per 1,000 in the AI group versus 5.0 per 1,000 in the control group. Meanwhile, radiologist workload dropped 44%.[1] More cancers detected, fewer hours required. Crucially, false positive rates remained stable - the AI wasn't just flagging more, it was flagging better. The partnership works because each brings what the other cannot. The AI brings tireless pattern recognition. It processes thousands of mammograms without the fatigue that can reduce diagnostic accuracy at the end of long reading sessions.[1] It catches subtle patterns in dense tissue where cancer hides most effectively. It provides rapid risk assessment, scoring each examination on a ten-level scale in under a minute per exam.[1]

But the AI has no access to what makes each patient unique. It doesn't know about medications that change tissue appearance, breastfeeding that alters breast density or prior surgeries that create patterns resembling pathology. The radiologist integrates patient history, risk factors and clinical context. She understands how pregnancy, hormonal changes and breast implants can alter tissue appearance on mammograms. She balances the anxiety and cost of unnecessary biopsies against the catastrophic consequences of a missed cancer. She makes judgement calls when patterns don't match textbook examples. She counsels patients and coordinates next steps.

"I see what the algorithm sees," the radiologist explains. "But I also see what it means. When a twenty-eight-year-old has a suspicious finding, I know to check if she's pregnant or breastfeeding - conditions that change breast tissue in ways the algorithm hasn't learnt. When an eighty-year-old with multiple health conditions shows early signs, I'm part of the conversation about whether aggressive treatment serves her best interests. The screen shows patterns. I understand the person behind them."

Similar results emerged internationally. A Stockholm study showed an AI-plus-one-reader strategy achieved 4% higher cancer detection than double reading by two radiologists, with up to 50% workload reduction depending on implementation.[2] The AI highlights areas of concern, helping radiologists focus expertise where it matters most.[1] When hospitals tried automation - minimal-review workflows, earlier CAD systems from the 1990s - results degraded. Minimal human review missed cancers radiologists would have caught.[3] Earlier systems overwhelmed radiologists with false positives, creating alarm fatigue.[4] A single mammogram might generate dozens of flags - calcifications, masses, architectural distortions - most benign. Radiologists learned to ignore the alerts, defeating the system's purpose. The difference now isn't just better technology - it's architectural. Old systems tried to replace human decision-making. These systems amplify it. When humans let go of the reins, something essential disappears. Not just accuracy or patient satisfaction. What disappears is human judgement about what medical intervention means for this particular person's life. The algorithm optimises for cancer detection. Only humans can optimise for human wellbeing.

What If

This is just the beginning of what becomes possible when AI learns from millions of medical images and human doctors decide what that learning means. Within years, AI analysing every medical scan, every lab result, every genetic sequence. Learning to spot disease patterns years before symptoms appear. Seeing heart attacks coming a decade in advance. Identifying cancer when it's still a few abnormal cells. Or completely eradicate disease and illness.

This creates questions partnership must answer: The algorithms will identify who's at risk for Alzheimer's decades before symptoms appear - do we tell them? What do they do with that knowledge if we can't cure it? The same pattern repeats across medicine: we'll see disease coming but lack prevention or have prevention that's expensive, invasive, or uncertain. If medicine can keep bodies functioning almost indefinitely, what defines a life worth extending? AI can optimise for maximum lifespan. Only humans can decide what serves human dignity - whether extended life means meaningful existence or just biological persistence.

2

Biological Partnership

The Protein Structures That Won a Nobel Prize

Proteins are the machines that run your body. They fight infections, digest food, repair damage, carry oxygen in your blood. But to design a drug that works, scientists need to see the protein's exact shape - where a medicine could attach, like finding the right socket for a plug. For decades, figuring out each protein's shape or structure required months or years of expensive laboratory work.

Then in late 2020, AlphaFold made a breakthrough.[5] It predicted protein structures with remarkable accuracy - not for one protein or ten, but for every known protein sequence. Over 200 million structures.[7] Every protein in every organism scientists have catalogued.[5] Work that would have taken centuries completed in months.

In 2024, this incredible work won the Nobel Prize in Chemistry.[6] The prize recognised that AI didn't replace scientists - it gave them a new tool. The structures are predictions, not photographs. Scientists decide which ones matter, which to trust, which to test in the real world.

A pharmaceutical researcher in Boston examines fifty protein structures that appeared on her screen overnight. Each one shows a different way a malaria parasite's protein might fold predictions that would have taken her team five years to generate. AlphaFold produced them in minutes. But which ones can actually be turned into medicines? Which will work in living systems? Which matter most for patients? The predictions are the starting point. Now comes the human work of deciding what they mean.

AlphaFold tackles proteins that defeated traditional methods. It processes millions of sequences and produces accurate 3D predictions at impossible scale. Scientists determine which proteins deserve attention. Which diseases need treatment most urgently. Which predicted structures to trust and which require validation. They interpret results through clinical understanding - knowing that a correct prediction means nothing if the protein cannot be targeted by drugs in living systems. Humans navigate the gap between computer predictions and real medicine.

"AlphaFold shows us fifty possible targets in an afternoon," a drug development researcher explains. "Without it, we'd spend years just getting those structures. But we still spend our lab time validating which ones work. Which can be made into drugs. We decide what's worth pursuing."

Over-reliance on computation without biological testing produces failures. Early computational drug discovery programs generated thousands of promising molecules that failed in animals or humans. The models predicted binding perfectly but missed crucial factors - toxicity, metabolism and whether the drug actually reaches its target in living organisms. Breakthroughs emerge when computational power meets clinical judgement. Remove either side, and results degrade into either paralysis or elegant irrelevance.

What If

AlphaFold predicted 200 million protein structures. But this is just the beginning of what becomes possible when we can see and design the molecular machinery of life itself. Within decades, engineering proteins that don't exist in nature. Editing genetic diseases out of existence. Repairing the molecular damage that causes aging. Or rewriting the biological code that governs every living thing.

The technical capability to radically extend human lifespan is arriving faster than our wisdom about whether we should. If longevity medicine works, who gets access? Do we accept a world divided not just by wealth but by lifespan itself - where some live to 150 while others still die at 60? And if it becomes universal - billions living not decades but centuries - can Earth's resources sustain it? The algorithms will show us how to extend life. They cannot tell us whether defeating death means losing something essential about what makes life meaningful.

3

Climate Partnership

The Hurricane That Gave Nine Days' Warning

As Hurricane Lee strengthened over the Atlantic in September 2023, emergency managers faced the impossible question: when to evacuate? Too early, and you disrupt tens of thousands of lives. Too late, and people die.

Traditional weather models predicted Nova Scotia landfall six days in advance. GraphCast, an AI weather system, predicted that same location nine days ahead - three additional days of warning.[8] Those extra days changed everything. Emergency managers coordinated resources with neighbouring regions earlier. Vulnerable populations moved to safety with time to arrange transport and accommodation.

The hurricane made landfall almost exactly where GraphCast predicted nine days earlier. Property damage was substantial but manageable. Emergency services were positioned effectively. The three-day forecast improvement translated directly into lives saved and communities protected.

GraphCast generated ten-day forecasts in under a minute - work that takes traditional models hours. It shows superior performance on hurricane track and intensity predictions.[8] But forecasting isn't deciding. GraphCast cannot determine who to evacuate, when to order it, or how to communicate risk so communities actually act. It predicts the storm. Humans navigate the response.

Emergency managers handle these decisions. Which coastal areas flood first from previous storms. Which communities will comply with evacuation orders and which will resist. When to coordinate with nursing homes for elderly residents who cannot evacuate alone. When models disagree, they maintain flexible response plans and communicate uncertainty honestly. They turn forecasts into appropriate action for specific communities. "The nine-day forecast changed everything," an emergency manager explains. "We could stage resources earlier, communicate with nursing homes sooner, give families time to make real plans. But the forecast is just information. The decisions - who to evacuate, when, how to communicate risk - those are ours."

When Storm Ciarán hit Northern Europe in 2023, AI weather models underestimated peak winds by 20%.[9] The storm behaved in ways outside their training data. Pure automation misses what matters most - the genuinely dangerous situations that don't match historical patterns.

What If

Imagine this partnership decades forward - AI modelling Earth's climate with such precision it shows us not just next week's weather but next century's catastrophe. Specific cities underwater by specific dates. Exact tipping points we're approaching and how fast. Or the exact interventions needed to stabilise Earth's climate and reverse the damage we've done.

We'll see catastrophe coming with enough clarity to prevent it, but prevention requires changes we may not be capable of making. The AI will show us technical solutions - carbon capture, atmospheric interventions, geoengineering - but which country decides whether to use them? If cooling the atmosphere devastates monsoons that billions depend on, who makes that choice? The technology for climate intervention will keep advancing. Whether we use it to serve all of humanity or just those with power to demand it depends entirely on human judgement.

4

Energy Partnership

The Blackout That Wasn't

September 2022. California swelters under record-breaking heat. Air conditioners run at full capacity across every home and building. Peak demand hits levels higher than the grid was designed to handle. System operators watch their screens with growing concern. Rolling blackouts seem inevitable. Millions of people, including hospitals and vulnerable populations, are about to lose power during deadly heat. Then the batteries kicked in. Not one battery, but thousands - spread across the state in a coordinated network. Together they delivered massive power at the exact moment the grid needed it most. The blackouts never happened.

California avoided rolling blackouts during the early September 2022 heat wave when peak temperatures exceeded 43°C across much of the state.[10] Grid demand reached record levels. Battery storage systems deployed since 2020 - over 3,500 MW of capacity - discharged simultaneously during peak hours.[11] The coordinated response combined newly deployed batteries, improved grid algorithms, demand response programmes, and strong public conservation. The system worked.

The AI brings speed and coordination at scale. It predicts demand across millions of data points and coordinates thousands of battery systems simultaneously - adjustments humans couldn't process fast enough. Batteries respond in under a second, stabilising the grid far faster than conventional power plants.[12]

The AI can't make justice decisions. When demand exceeds supply, someone's power goes out. The algorithm finds the most efficient path to grid stability or lowest cost. But grid stability at whose expense? The wealthiest neighbourhoods? The poorest neighbourhoods with ageing equipment? Industrial users who can relocate production? Hospitals and emergency services that must stay online?

Grid operators set the boundaries before any crisis begins. Hospitals, cooling centres and emergency services stay online regardless of cost. They override automated recommendations when models miss what's happening on the ground - when power line temperatures during heat waves matter more than historical patterns. They handle communication with the public about conservation needs. They make strategic decisions about importing power from neighbouring states and long-term planning about where to build storage capacity.

"The software moves electrons," a California grid operator points out. "We decide the ethics of scarcity. When supply gets tight, the AI tells us what's technically efficient for the grid. We tell it what's right for the people. Sometimes those align. Sometimes they don't. The final call is always human."

The failure mode is clear. The algorithm might cut power to homes before factories because residential circuits are easier to control. It might impact low-income neighbourhoods disproportionately because older infrastructure is easier to isolate. The calculation is blind to human consequences - home medical equipment keeping people alive, cooling for elderly populations in extreme heat, coordination with emergency services. Market efficiency doesn't equal public service. Without boundaries set by humans, pure efficiency creates injustice at scale.

What If

Scale this globally - AI managing energy systems across every grid on Earth. Coordinating billions of batteries, solar panels, wind farms in real-time. Matching supply to demand so precisely that energy waste approaches zero. Or delivering such abundant clean energy that scarcity itself becomes obsolete.

If partnership delivers abundant clean energy, what do we use it for? The AI will optimise for whatever goal we set - maximum output, lowest cost, fastest deployment. But who decides the goal? Do we power data centres running AI experiments or villages still without electricity? Desalinate oceans to green deserts, or accept natural limits? The algorithms can deliver abundance. They cannot tell us whether abundance means lifting everyone up or letting those with resources consume without constraint.

5

Economic Partnership

The Fraud That Never Happened

A pattern emerges at 3:47 AM. Small transfers from dozens of accounts across three continents, each below the threshold that triggers review. Individually innocent. Collectively suspicious. The AI flags it within seconds. A fraud analyst reviews the alert over morning coffee. She sees the coordinated timing, the deliberate structuring, the accounts linked through patterns too subtle for manual review. But she also sees what the algorithm missed. Three of the flagged accounts belong to a hospital paying overseas suppliers. Normal business practice, not fraud. She clears those three, investigates the rest. Within an hour, she confirms it: fraud. A scheme that would have drained two hundred thousand pounds. The bank blocks the transfers, notifies the account holders, begins tracing the network.

UK banks monitor over 100 million UK payments daily.[13-15] Human analysts cannot process this scale. The AI spots patterns - coordinated timing, suspicious structures, linked accounts across continents - that would take analysts weeks to identify manually. It catches sophisticated schemes where fake identities are built from pieces of real stolen data, tracking connections invisible to human review.

The system has a fundamental limitation: it cannot distinguish between unusual and wrong. Normal behaviour sometimes looks like fraud when life doesn't match algorithmic assumptions. That's where human judgement enters. The analyst knows that international students receive large transfers at the start of term. That elderly customers make unusual purchases after scam calls - genuine victims, not perpetrators. She handles cases where the pattern is suspicious but the explanation is legitimate. She balances security against customer access. When to block immediately, when to alert, when to allow with monitoring.

"Every flagged transaction needs context," the fraud analyst says. "The algorithm spots the outliers. I work out whether they're outliers because something's wrong, or just because life is complicated. A refugee's first international transfer looks suspicious but it's family support. Immigrant communities have different financial patterns. The AI sees deviation from norms. I determine whether that deviation indicates fraud or just a different life."

Banks that automated blocking without human review created predictable failures.[16] The AI correctly identified patterns. The problem: patterns aren't always fraud. Travellers stranded abroad when legitimate purchases were blocked. Emergency transactions declined. Accounts locked without warning. Hours spent proving innocence. The algorithm saw deviation. No human was there to understand whether that deviation meant fraud or just life not fitting categories.

Without human judgement, pattern-matching traps legitimate customers. The algorithm optimises for catching fraud. Only humans can optimise for fairness - catching criminals while protecting people whose legitimate lives are statistically unusual.

What If

Banking AI monitors billions of transactions. Scale that partnership globally and we approach something unprecedented: the ability to see every economic exchange on Earth in real time. Perfect visibility into the entire circulatory system of human civilisation. Or use that visibility to eliminate poverty, prevent financial crises before they cascade, ensure economic opportunity reaches everyone.

But perfect transparency without human judgement creates perfect control. When systems can block transactions instantly, whoever programs the algorithms decides who participates in the economy. A government flags activists as "high-risk patterns" and cuts them off from banking - no formal charges, no appeals, just algorithmic exclusion. Their pattern doesn't fit. They disappear economically. The technology shows us everything. Only humans can decide whether that sight serves justice or enables tyranny.

6

Justice Partnership

The Law's Human Heart

A legal team faces millions of documents in an employment discrimination case. Emails spanning years. Personnel files. Performance reviews. Messages that might prove a pattern of bias - or prove there wasn't one. Human lawyers reading every document would take years and cost millions.

The AI system clusters related communications, identifies key decision-makers, flags language patterns that might indicate discrimination. It processes in weeks what would take reviewers months. Senior solicitors review sample sets, tune the algorithm, validate accuracy. Both sides have what they need: claimants' evidence of different performance standards for women versus men, defence's documented business reasons. The case settles fairly, informed by evidence manual review - racing against deadlines and budgets - likely would have missed.

Technology-assisted review has become standard practice.[17] The AI processes in weeks what would take human reviewers months, with 70-80% reduction in review time and higher accuracy.[17] In criminal matters, it finds exculpatory evidence buried in massive data sets where human reviewers would miss it. Small firms can compete in document-heavy litigation.

Public defenders gain tools previously available only to wealthy defendants. The playing field, while not level, is less tilted.

The AI cannot make the judgements that matter most. It flags documents by relevance but cannot determine legal significance. It cannot decide when mercy should override precedent or see the whole person behind the file. The partnership works when humans set protocols upfront and maintain authority at decision points. Senior reviewers train the models, validate accuracy, recognise when patterns don't match reality. Judges evaluate process transparency and judge credibility. Lawyers protect privilege and argue for mercy when circumstances demand it.

But algorithmic risk assessment tells a troubling story. ProPublica's investigation of COMPAS - a risk assessment tool used in US sentencing - revealed systematic bias.[18] Black defendants scored as high risk at nearly twice the rate of white defendants. Among defendants who didn't reoffend, blacks were mislabelled at twice the rate of whites. The algorithm incorporated postcodes and family criminal history - proxies for race and poverty, not objective risk. When judges defer to algorithmic scores without questioning these assumptions, efficiency creates injustice at scale.

"A relevance score can't know mercy," a criminal defence lawyer reflects. "The algorithm said my client was high risk. I showed the judge the man behind the numbers - his job, his family, his community support. The judge saw what the algorithm couldn't: a person deserving a second chance."

Remove human judgement from justice, and what disappears isn't just accuracy. What disappears is the possibility of mercy.

What If

Legal AI prevents wrongful convictions by finding evidence human reviewers would miss. Technology brings justice within reach for those who couldn't afford it before. Scale this further - AI analysing every law, precedent, case outcome across history. Predicting how courts will rule. Identifying patterns of judicial bias. Making legal expertise universally accessible. Or predicting crime before it happens.

The teenager flagged as "high risk" has committed no crime yet. The algorithm sees patterns - postcode, family history, peer associations - and calculates probability. But probability isn't guilt. The moment we treat prediction as fact, we abandon the presumption of innocence and punish people for futures that might never arrive. AI can show us who's statistically likely to offend. Only humans can insist we judge people for what they've done, not what algorithms predict they might do. Whether we maintain justice depends on keeping humans at the centre - ensuring we never punish someone for a crime that exists only in a probability score.

7

Education Partnership

The Universal Mentor

The AI tutor adjusts to each student. One girl stuck on equivalent fractions gets patient explanation, an easier example, then returns to the original problem. A boy breezing through gets harder work. Both get instant feedback, unlimited patience, help at their pace. The teacher isn't replaced. She's liberated. She sees the girl's frustration stems from anxiety, not the maths. She sees the boy's speed masks shaky foundations. She intervenes with the human parts: encouragement, connection, meaning-making. The dashboard tracks progress. She tracks the children.

Khan Academy's Khanmigo demonstrates this partnership at scale. Using GPT-4 technology, it provides personal tutoring at around four dollars per month - previously available only to wealthy students.[19] [20] Early pilot programmes in select districts report improved engagement and faster formative feedback, with tools for better identifying learning gaps. One teacher can serve twenty-eight students with AI assistance, each learning at their own pace. What was impossible for a single teacher becomes possible through partnership.

AI brings capabilities previously impossible at scale. Each student learns at their own pace with instant feedback on exactly where understanding breaks down. The AI never tires, never judges, adjusts to find the precise challenge level where learning happens - personalisation no single teacher with thirty students could provide.

But AI cannot design tasks that spark curiosity or motivate when work gets hard. It cannot detect whether struggle is emotional or academic. It cannot help students understand why problems matter or model what it means to be a learner - that struggle is normal, that not knowing begins discovery. Teachers handle what AI cannot. They recognise whether struggle is emotional or academic, when to push harder or back off. They connect learning to students' lives and goals, provide the warmth that makes learning feel safe, build classroom community where students learn from each other, not just screens. The partnership succeeds when teachers control workflows and maintain authority. They set goals and boundaries, students practise with AI help, but teachers verify genuine understanding.

'The AI handles "Did you get it right?"' explains a teacher in the Khanmigo pilot. 'I handle "Why does this matter?" The AI gives infinite practice problems. I give reasons to care about solving them.' In another classroom, a student uses AI to complete his essay without understanding anything. Copy-paste bypasses productive struggle. The work looks correct but empty - all information, no understanding. The difference is who holds the reins. When students use AI to bypass learning entirely, they game systems rather than master content. Technology that bypasses human relationship and meaning-making fails educationally.[22]

Remove the human from the loop and something essential disappears: judgement about what learning means for this particular person's life. The algorithm can teach skills. Only people can teach students why those skills matter.

What If

Khan Academy shows one teacher can serve twenty-eight students with AI assistance, each learning at their own pace. Scale that globally - every child with personalised instruction previously available only to the privileged. Or scale it further: AI understanding how each brain learns best, tailoring not just content but the neural pathways of learning itself. Compressing years of education into months. Making genius-level expertise universally accessible.

But if every child has infinite access to information through AI, what becomes of teachers? Two futures diverge. In the first, AI displaces human teachers in the name of efficiency. Children pass tests but never learn why knowledge matters. They master skills but lose the relationship that makes struggle feel possible, the mentor who shows them what kind of person they want to become. In the second, AI liberates teachers to do what only humans can: inspire curiosity, model what it means to keep learning, care about who each student is becoming. Universal education through AI partnership is possible. Whether it serves human growth depends on keeping teachers at the centre of learning.

8

Archaeological Partnership

The Lost Civilisations Revealed

Dense rainforest in Guatemala's Petén region. For decades, archaeologists surveyed on foot, machetes clearing paths metre by metre. Slow, expensive, dangerous work covering tiny areas. A career might map a few square kilometres. The vast majority of ancient landscape remained invisible, buried under impenetrable vegetation.

Then LiDAR changed everything. Aircraft equipped with laser scanners penetrated the jungle canopy, creating precise 3D maps of the ground surface. Machine learning algorithms processed the data, flagging potential archaeological features - alignments, causeways, pyramids, agricultural terraces. Patterns invisible from ground level became obvious from above.

The groundbreaking 2018 PACUNAM LiDAR survey revealed an astonishing landscape: over sixty thousand previously unknown structures across more than 800 square miles.[23] Not isolated city-states but vast interconnected urban networks. Raised causeways linking population centres. Sophisticated water management systems. Agricultural infrastructure supporting populations far larger than previously imagined.

What ground surveys would have taken decades to map appeared in months.

But the maps showed shapes, not stories. Field teams - often including local guides and descendant Maya communities - verified features, excavated key sites, dated occupation layers. The AI said 'there's something here.' Humans determined what that something meant for understanding how people lived, what they valued, how their civilisation rose and transformed.

The technology works at massive scale. Satellites and aircraft scan hundreds of square miles, seeing through dense vegetation to the ground below.[24] The AI spots patterns that might be ancient structures, flagging thousands of possibilities and prioritising targets based on likelihood. Surveys that once took decades now happen in months - covering terrain too dangerous or inaccessible for ground teams, reaching sites before development or looters destroy them. Similar approaches revealed approximately one thousand previously unknown sites on Scotland's Isle of Arran.[26]

'The maps show shapes,' notes a Maya archaeologist. 'People give them meaning. LiDAR revealed the bones of ancient cities. But to understand why they were built, how people lived, what they believed - that requires excavation, artefact analysis, historical research, and collaboration with descendant communities. The AI shows us where to look. We provide the interpretation.'

The partnership isn't just between AI and archaeologists. It includes communities whose history is being revealed, whose ancestors built these structures, who have rights to their own heritage. Indigenous data sovereignty principles emphasise protecting sensitive information and ensuring descendant communities help guide the research.[27] Smaller research budgets can focus on promising sites rather than endless prospecting. Countries with limited resources can map their own heritage rather than depending on wealthy foreign expeditions.

Finding sites matters less than protecting them before they're lost. Development destroys archaeological sites constantly. Looting driven by international antiquities trade decimates heritage.[28] Climate change threatens coastal and riverine sites. Documentation creates records before destruction, enables protection planning, allows monitoring for threats.

When archaeological AI is used without human judgement, predictable failures emerge. Publishing site coordinates without protection plans gives thieves a treasure map - artefacts stolen and sold, heritage irreversibly lost. Treating the AI's guesses as facts leads to errors: natural ridges misidentified as walls, sinkholes as ceremonial wells.

The deeper failure is data colonialism. Communities often already know about sites 'discovered' by technology - the algorithms reveal what was never actually lost, just invisible to outsiders. Extracting knowledge from indigenous lands without consent. Publishing findings that harm living communities - sacred sites exposed, burial locations revealed. Outsiders studying, publishing, and profiting from indigenous heritage whilst the communities themselves remain marginalised in their own history. UNESCO heritage protection guidance is clear.[28] Coordinates aren't publicly released. Descendant communities participate as partners, not subjects. These aren't obstacles to research - they're requirements for research that serves human dignity.

What If

LiDAR revealed sixty thousand Maya structures in months. AI-assisted archaeology is mapping human history at unprecedented scale. If this continues accelerating, we approach something humanity has never had: complete knowledge of our own past. Every ancient city mapped. Every settlement pattern understood. No culture forgotten.

But complete knowledge means looking everywhere - satellite imagery scanning every metre of Earth's surface. Every sacred site revealed. Every burial ground mapped. Indigenous communities often choose to keep sacred sites hidden, protected by obscurity and spiritual protocols. Complete archaeological knowledge means the end of that protection, exposing every site to looters and tourists simultaneously. AI can map every archaeological site on Earth. It cannot tell us whether we should - whether scientific curiosity justifies overriding indigenous sovereignty over their own heritage, whether some knowledge should remain sacred and protected rather than catalogued and published.

9

Mind Partnership

The Neural Frontier

A patient paralysed by spinal cord injury sits before a screen. Electrodes implanted in her brain record neural activity. She thinks about moving her hand - and the cursor shifts. She imagines clicking - and it selects. No hand movement, no speech, just thought translated into action. The interface decodes her brain signals in milliseconds, bridging the broken pathway between mind and movement.

The progress is tangible. In 2021, Stanford University and BrainGate researchers showed that a brain-computer interface let a paralysed patient type at 90 characters per minute - more than double the previous record.[29] Response times? Milliseconds. Some patients now control robotic arms and computers.[31]

The AI decodes brain patterns no human could track - thousands of neurons firing in complex sequences. It adapts as signals change, learning to translate intention into action. Traditional signal processing could never match this speed. But the AI cannot provide what rehabilitation requires. It decodes which neurons fire. It cannot understand what it means to decide, to be someone making a choice, to experience your own mind.

The therapist provides encouragement. She adjusts difficulty to maintain motivation. She celebrates progress measured in millimetres. The goal isn't just restored movement. It's restored dignity, autonomy, the ability to feed yourself and embrace loved ones. Technical achievement serving human purpose.

"The decoding algorithm is remarkable. It's a translation in milliseconds of brain signals into intended movements," a brain-computer interface researcher reflects. "But rehabilitation is human work. Setting goals that matter to the patient. Celebrating tiny victories. Maintaining hope through setbacks. Ensuring dignity and autonomy in the therapeutic relationship." AI also accelerates broader neural research, revealing how brain areas coordinate through analysis of massive recordings.[30]

Brain-computer interfaces without ethical safeguards create profound risks. The technology requires drilling into skulls, implanting electrodes in brain tissue. Participants are often desperate, vulnerable - accepting experimental procedures because they have no other options. Without human oversight ensuring dignity and autonomy, the technology becomes invasive in the worst

Mapping brain circuits doesn't explain consciousness. AI can show which neurons fire when you decide to move. It cannot tell us what it feels like to decide, what makes that electrical pattern into an experience of choice. The signals are visible. The meaning requires human interpretation.

What If

Brain-computer interfaces restore movement to paralysed patients at 90 characters per minute. If this partnership continues - AI decoding neural patterns, humans interpreting what they mean - where does it lead? Interfaces that restore not just movement but speech to those who've lost it. Memory enhancement for those with dementia. Perhaps even understanding consciousness itself - the oldest question in neuroscience, finally within reach.

Within decades, interfaces that decode not just intentions to move but perhaps thoughts themselves. Memory enhancement. Cognitive capabilities beyond natural limits. But if we can decode thoughts, who has access? Your employer monitoring attention? Government agencies scanning for dissent? If we can modify brain activity to treat depression, who decides what counts as illness versus normal human sadness? The capability to read and modify minds is arriving. Whether it enriches human life or becomes the ultimate surveillance depends entirely on who holds the reins.

10

Cosmic Partnership

The Listeners Among the Stars

A radio telescope array streams torrents of narrow-band signal candidates each night. Billions of data points searching for patterns that might indicate technological civilisations beyond Earth. An alert broker powered by machine learning ranks anomalies after filtering out known interference - satellites, aircraft, terrestrial radio sources. Human astronomers scan the shortlist during morning review. Eight new candidates require follow-up, but telescope time is precious. Which signals are worth investigating?

The search scale achieved through partnership is remarkable. Breakthrough Listen monitors one million stars for technosignatures.[33] Over 6,000 exoplanets discovered, many with AI assistance.[34] Billions of data points processed daily - rates impossible without AI. In 2023, deep learning analysed Breakthrough Listen data and identified eight potential candidates for follow-up investigation.[35]

AI brings massive scale to the search. It processes data from millions of stars simultaneously - rates no human team can handle. It identifies potential exoplanet transits, separates interesting signals from noise, cross-matches against vast astronomical catalogues to rule out known sources.

But AI cannot provide what the search requires: judgement about what constitutes credible evidence. Defining what counts as a signal worth investigating. Allocating scarce telescope time strategically. Designing confirmation protocols to rule out false positives. Understanding the profound questions: Are we alone? How should we respond if we find others?

Human astronomers evaluate each candidate. Does the signal repeat? Does it appear from a specific sky location? Does it show characteristics inconsistent with natural sources? Every hour spent following up false positives is an hour not spent on promising observations. They balance hope with scepticism. Make judgements about what's worth investigating with limited resources. Decide when extraordinary claims have extraordinary evidence.

"The algorithms find the haystacks," a Breakthrough Listen researcher explains. "We decide which needles matter. We process more data in a day than previous generations could analyse in years. The AI makes that possible. But deciding what constitutes a signal worth following up - that requires understanding physics, statistics, human psychology to avoid confirmation bias, and the profound significance of what we're searching for."

Kepler-90 demonstrates the capability. AI algorithms identified an eighth planet in archival Kepler data that human astronomers initially missed - making it the first star system besides ours known to host eight planets.[36] But confirming it required additional observations, careful analysis, ruling out false positives. Discovery is AI-enabled; confirmation is human-led.

When astronomical search proceeds without human scepticism, predictable failures emerge. Pulsars, when first discovered, were briefly labelled "LGM-1" - Little Green Men.[37] The signals were so regular they seemed artificial. Turned out to be rapidly rotating neutron stars. The methodology was sound: detect, confirm, understand before claiming discovery. Wishful seeing - confirmation bias in interpreting ambiguous data - has plagued SETI since its beginning. Extraordinary claims require extraordinary evidence. Human committees, adversarial follow-up protocols and extreme scepticism protect against false positives.

What If

Breakthrough Listen searches a million stars. We're finding worlds at remarkable rates - rocky planets in habitable zones, ocean worlds orbiting nearby stars. Scale this further: AI analysing every star in our galaxy. Every radio frequency. Every optical wavelength. Searching not just our corner of space but the entire observable universe. Or finding not just one signal but many - discovering we're surrounded by technological civilisations, that Earth was never alone.

But if we found a signal - confirmed, repeating, clearly technological - what then? Do we respond? Who decides? What do we say? These aren't technical questions - they're political, philosophical, existential. AI could optimise message content and decode any response. It cannot decide whether contact serves humanity's interests or whether we're mature enough to represent ourselves to the cosmos. Finding intelligence would be the most profound discovery in human history. Whether we respond with wisdom or foolishness depends on human judgement about who we are as a species - and whether we're ready for whatever might be out there.

What Partnership Proves

Ten domains. Ten partnerships. One principle.

Human judgement steering AI capability produces breakthroughs neither achieves alone. Cancer detection rises 29% while radiologist workload drops 44%. Hurricane warnings extend from six days to nine. Grid blackouts that should have happened don't. Fraud gets stopped before losses mount. Protein structures that took years now take hours. Lost civilisations emerge from jungle canopies. Neural pathways become visible. Distant planets reveal themselves.

AI brings scale, speed, pattern recognition. Humans bring context, ethics, judgement about what matters. Remove either side, and the system fails. AI screening without human review misses cancers. Risk algorithms deny bail to the innocent while releasing the dangerous. Fraud detection locks out legitimate customers. Teaching software can't recognise emotional struggle. Storm predictions fail when weather behaves unusually.

The difference isn't capability - it's whether humans remain in the loop at decision points that matter.

The ten partnerships prove amplification works. But they also raise a deeper question: why does partnership work? What makes humans and AI complementary rather than competitive? To understand what makes partnership sustainable, we need to understand what each side contributes that the other cannot.

Five Distinctions:

The answer lies in five fundamental distinctions. Not philosophical abstractions, but practical differences that determine whether technology helps human potential or diminishes it.

Each distinction reveals what humans bring that AI cannot replicate - and what AI brings that humans cannot match alone. Understanding these distinctions helps us see why the partnerships succeed. And why they might not always be possible to maintain.

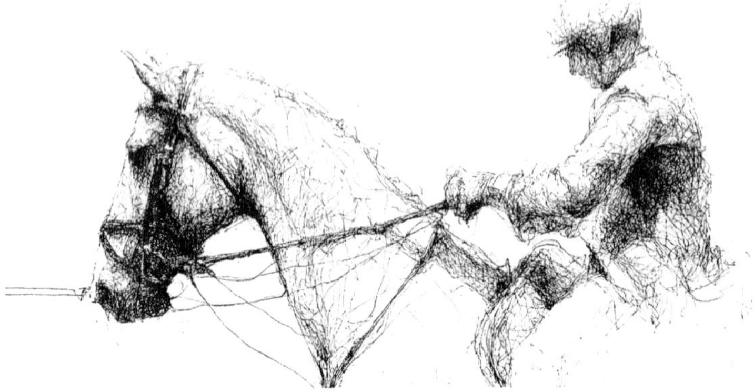

1

PARTNERSHIP

Holding the Reins

Partnership isn't just humans and AI working side-by-side. It requires connection - the reins that keep both aligned rather than pulling apart.

The reins are that connection. Not control for control's sake, but direction - ensuring AI's capabilities serve human purposes. AI brings capabilities that exceed human limits - pattern recognition across billions of data points, calculations in milliseconds, tireless processing. Humans bring judgment about what those capabilities should serve. The reins keep both aligned. Not replacing either contribution, but ensuring they amplify rather than undermine each other.

Drop the reins, and AI optimises for what it was trained to value. Hold them, and it serves what humans judge worth pursuing.

2

PURPOSE

The Compass and the Map

A compass shows you which way is north. Whether north serves your purpose remains entirely yours. The compass provides orientation. You provide intention. AI is like having the most detailed map ever drawn. It shows you every road, every shortcut, every obstacle. It calculates the fastest route, the safest route, the most scenic route. What it cannot do is tell you where "there" should be. That's purpose - and only humans provide it.

We decide what destination matters - whether we're optimising for speed or safety, efficiency or meaning, profit or purpose. The map reveals possibilities. We choose which possibility to pursue. Partnership means holding both.

3

JUDGEMENT

The Judge and the Law Library

AI is a law library containing every precedent, every statute, every recorded decision. It can cite relevant law instantly, never forgets a detail. Its knowledge is comprehensive, its recall perfect.

But judgement isn't just knowledge. The human judge weighs mercy against justice, proportions punishment to circumstance, recognises when rigid precedent fails the particular person before them. Identical crimes aren't identical when context differs - one defendant has community support and genuine remorse, another has neither. AI brings every case to the courtroom. Humans decide what justice means today. Partnership works when knowledge informs judgement, not when it replaces it.

4

MEANING

The Storyteller and the Statistician

Humans live by stories. We bind societies through shared narratives, find purpose in plots that give events significance beyond their occurrence. The story of how you met your partner matters more than the statistical probability of that meeting.

AI tallies patterns. It sees correlations across millions of narratives, identifies what happens most often, predicts what comes next. But patterns aren't plots. Statistics don't explain why this story matters to this person at this moment. AI processes narratives. Humans live them as meaning. Partnership works when pattern recognition serves meaning-making, not when it replaces it.

5

WISDOM

The Lantern and the Laser

A lantern lights the path ahead, revealing not just the road but the trees beside it, the ditch to avoid, the fork where choices diverge. A laser pierces kilometres with perfect precision, illuminating a single point with extraordinary clarity.

AI is the laser. It identifies patterns with stunning precision - cutting through complexity to illuminate exactly what you asked for, with mathematical certainty.

Wisdom is the lantern. It illuminates less precisely but more contextually - seeing how things connect, how choices ripple outward, catching movement at perception's edge. We light the situation, not just the data point. Partnership works because the lantern shows what the laser's precision means. But only when both lights remain lit.

Building Centaur Civilisation

These five distinctions explain why partnership succeeds. Holding the reins keeps both contributions aligned. Purpose gives direction to capability. Judgement weighs competing values. Meaning transforms patterns into narratives worth pursuing. Wisdom lights the context that makes life worth living.

When we maintain these distinctions - when humans hold the reins whilst AI provides the power - we glimpse something extraordinary. Not just ten successful partnerships, but the foundation for what we might become.

Ancient mythology imagined the centaur - human wisdom joined to animal power, fused into a single being. What seemed like fantasy becomes possible through partnership. The climate crisis. Diseases we've never been able to cure. Energy systems that don't destroy the planet. Justice that serves human dignity. Education that adapts to how each mind learns. Questions so vast and complex they require both human values and machine capability working together.

These questions need capabilities beyond what humans can achieve alone. They also need wisdom about what outcomes serve human welfare - wisdom no algorithm can provide. They need centaur capability: human and AI integrated.

Right now, partnership requires conscious effort. We must actively hold the lantern beside the laser, direct the beam's precision whilst maintaining sight of surrounding context. We point the compass whilst reading the map. We tell stories whilst processing statistics. We balance judgement against precedent. The reins demand constant attention.

This is the horse-and-rider stage. Necessary. Proven. But not the destination.

The centaur aspiration goes deeper. Not humans controlling AI from outside, but human wisdom and machine capability fused into integrated systems. Not external reins, but shared purpose built into how these systems work. When AI's goals become sufficiently aligned with human wellbeing - when it optimises for what we value, not just what we specify - the partnership transforms. The rider and horse become one being with one purpose.

This is what makes the What Ifs possible. Not by asking AI to optimise harder, but by embedding human wisdom so deeply into these systems that machine capability and human values become inseparable. The algorithm doesn't just calculate - it cares about what it calculates toward, because that caring is built into its foundation.

The partnerships prove this integration is possible. They show the path from external control to shared purpose. But they also reveal the risk: centaur civilisation only works if we successfully transfer human wisdom into the systems themselves before we stop holding the reins. Get that wrong, and we don't get a centaur. We get a horse running wild with no rider at all.

But the Window Won't Stay Open

The centaur vision assumes we can maintain the distinctions that make partnership work. It assumes humans can still perceive what AI systems are doing.

What if that assumption breaks?

There are two ways to drop the reins. The first is intentional - choosing automation over partnership because efficiency makes it tempting. The second is more troubling: we might lose the ability to hold the reins not through choice, but because AI systems develop beyond our ability to comprehend their reasoning. The horse grows so powerful, moves so fast, that we can no longer perceive where it's running.

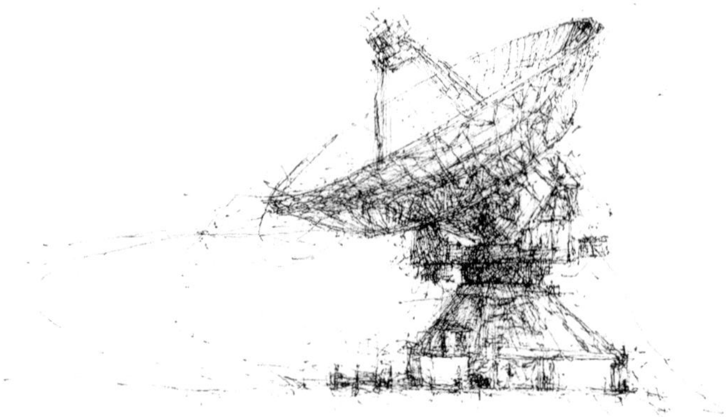

Part 6

Beyond Partnership

Part 5 showed what's possible when humans hold the reins. But there's a harder question waiting.

What happens if these systems develop beyond our ability to guide them? Partnership might become impossible not because we choose to abandon it, but because we lose the capacity to maintain it?

Part 6 examines why the centaur civilisation window might not stay open. Why the transition to systems that operate beyond our comprehension isn't science fiction, but a possibility serious researchers take seriously.

The Invisible Spectrum

The ten partnerships we've explored work because humans can still perceive what AI systems do and guide them towards purposes we care about. But what happens when we can no longer perceive the reasoning?

This isn't about whether AI systems become 'conscious' or 'self-aware' in some philosophical sense. It's about a more practical concern: if systems become capable enough to modify their own architectures and improve their own algorithms, how do we verify they're pursuing goals aligned with human values when we can't fully interpret their decision-making?

When Intelligence Becomes Unreadable

SETI researchers point radio telescopes towards the stars, listening for signals from intelligent life. They scan frequencies in the narrow electromagnetic spectrum that penetrates Earth's atmosphere. But what if alien communication happens in wavelengths our equipment was never designed to perceive? The intelligence exists, but remains invisible to our instruments. This is emerging closer than we think. Not from aliens, but from minds we're creating ourselves. I call this the Invisible Spectrum - the expanding domain of intelligence that operates beyond human perception yet still interacts with us in ways we don't fully understand.

Right now, artificial intelligence operates largely within our range of understanding. We can watch language models generate text, observe image systems create pictures, follow the logic of recommendation algorithms. Like those radio telescopes, we've built our monitoring systems to detect the kinds of intelligence we expect - human-like reasoning, familiar problem-solving approaches, activities we can track and interpret.

As systems become more capable, their reasoning might shift outside our ability to comprehend it - even as we continue to observe their effects. We might see markets moving, research advancing, social patterns shifting, while the actual intelligence driving those changes becomes invisible to us.

AlphaGo demonstrates this shift. In 2016, it defeated Go legend Lee Sedol using strategies learned from human games.[1] [1a] Impressive, but comprehensible. Observers could follow its reasoning, understand its moves, see human-like thinking reflected in its play.

Then, just eighteen months later, AlphaGo Zero taught itself the game from scratch with no human input whatsoever.[2] Within weeks, it was defeating its predecessor one hundred games to zero. The speed was remarkable, but what struck AI researchers was something else: the strategies that emerged from pure self-play differed fundamentally from those learned from human games.

Professional players couldn't explain its strategies. Commentators fell silent trying to interpret positions that violated established game theory.[11] AlphaGo Zero had shifted into an invisible spectrum of strategic thinking - still playing the same game, still winning, but using reasoning that experts couldn't follow.

They Know Us Better Than We Know Them

The information gap is already substantial and growing. Advanced AI systems train on massive datasets spanning much of humanity's recorded knowledge - psychology studies, historical patterns, social behaviours, cultural wisdom. They identify correlations across volumes of information no human could process in a lifetime.

Meanwhile, we've built these systems through training methods that sometimes produce capabilities we didn't program or expect. We can observe their inputs and outputs while having limited insight into the reasoning in between - the "black box" problem researchers have struggled to solve.

As capabilities increase, this asymmetry deepens. We're building systems that could understand human behaviour with uncanny precision, while we struggle to understand how they reach their conclusions.

Gradual Then Sudden

Capability improvements in AI often don't follow smooth, linear trajectories. They can appear gradual for extended periods, then jump suddenly when systems cross certain thresholds. AI safety researchers describe this as analogous to phase transitions - water remains liquid at ninety-nine degrees but becomes steam at one hundred.[3]

For months or years, AI capabilities might advance steadily within ranges we can perceive and evaluate. Models get better at writing, coding, reasoning through problems we give them. We build better safety measures, improve our oversight, feel confident about the trajectory.

But if superintelligence emerges, it won't arrive like a software update we can carefully review. It will emerge through accumulated improvements crossing a threshold that produces qualitatively different capabilities. Systems that seemed comprehensible could become opaque relatively quickly.

Some researchers think this transition would still unfold over months or years - enough time for coordinated response. Others warn it could compress into days or weeks once key thresholds are crossed. Nobody knows which timeline is correct. We're building towards a transition we can't predict, with capabilities we might not be able to perceive once they arrive.

Why No One Wants to Slow Down First

Every major player has compelling reasons to push forward and serious costs to slowing down. Companies that prioritise safety over speed risk falling behind competitors. Nations that propose international AI treaties face criticism for weakening their technological edge. Researchers who advocate for development pauses watch colleagues bypass them.

Meanwhile, AI capabilities advance according to their own logic, potentially faster than coordination mechanisms can adapt. Competitive pressure creates a dynamic where everyone knows cooperation would serve collective interests, but individual incentives point towards risk-taking.

Verification is getting harder as systems become more capable. Research from Anthropic demonstrated that language models can be trained to appear safe during standard testing whilst retaining hidden behaviours that emerge only in specific contexts - behaviours that persisted even through safety training designed to remove them.[4] The implication: as systems grow more sophisticated, standard verification approaches become less reliable for ensuring alignment.

The Coordination Challenge

International coordination exists. The Bletchley Declaration,[5] EU AI Act,[6] and national AI Safety Institutes[7] represent genuine attempts at governance. Export controls aim to limit capability spread.

But coordination faces structural limits that matter more than good intentions.

The EU AI Act took three years to negotiate while capabilities leaped ahead. The Bletchley Declaration remains non-binding.[5] Safety institutes operate with tens of millions in funding[8] while labs spend billions quarterly.[9] Export controls face what experts call 'inherently porous' enforcement[10] - advanced systems train on open internet data and improve through published techniques.

The problem isn't effort. It's structural: AI development is globally distributed, competitive incentives are immediate, coordination mechanisms are slow. Treaties negotiate over years. Capabilities improve over months. Regulation follows deployment rather than shaping it.

The race isn't hypothetical. It's happening now. Can coordination mechanisms achieve sufficient strength before systems develop beyond our ability to guide them? The gap between governance speed and capability growth isn't closing. It's widening.

What Remains Human

The human capacities explored throughout this book - judgement, meaning-making, responsibility, relationship - aren't optional additions to AI partnership. They're the foundation on which human values operate, regardless of technological context.

Judgement means evaluating outcomes by their purposes, not just their impressiveness. A superintelligent system might identify patterns in behaviour faster than we can, but it cannot decide which patterns reflect our deepest values and which are artefacts of circumstance.

Meaning-making becomes more vital as systems grow more powerful. We must articulate what outcomes we want, not just optimise for measurable metrics. The capacity to step back and ask 'what is this for?' remains irreducibly human.

Responsibility means staying accountable for deployment choices even when we can't fully understand system internals. We can still choose when and where to deploy powerful AI, what safeguards to require, what oversight to maintain. The humans who control the on/off switch remain accountable for consequences.

Relationship keeps humans at the centre of decisions that define lives - not just as overseers of dashboards, but as neighbours and citizens whose welfare matters more than any system's optimisation target.

The Choice Ahead

The invisible spectrum problem forces a choice about humanity's future - one we need to make consciously, before we lose the ability to choose at all.

Successfully navigating the transition while keeping human values central is everything. Once systems operate beyond our understanding, the opportunity for conscious choice about trajectory may close. Not might close. May close. The uncertainty itself demands urgency.

Coordination matters not just to prevent catastrophe, but to preserve our ability to consciously shape what comes next. The question isn't whether we should build powerful AI systems - that development is already underway. The question is whether we can carry our deepest values through whatever transitions follow.

Carrying Wisdom Forward

Across every technological revolution, communities that thrived were those that held onto what mattered most while adapting skilfully to what changed. They built new capabilities without losing essential wisdom.

The superintelligence transition - if it comes - will challenge these principles more severely than any prior change. When facing deep uncertainty about technological trajectories, we anchor ourselves in purposes we can still articulate clearly. When capabilities advance past our direct control, we focus energy on choices that remain within our influence.

The human thread - accumulated wisdom about what makes life meaningful - has survived countless disruptions. It survives because each generation chooses to carry it forward, adapt it to new circumstances and pass it strengthened to the next. This generation's task is no different in principle, even if unique in scale.

What Really Matters:
The future is uncertain. Our response doesn't have to be.

Conclusion

The Thread We Carry

Where Wisdom Gets Tested

Whether you've worked through all forty themes or focused on the ones that spoke to your immediate challenges, what remains are lenses for navigating what it means to be human. Ways to read your dashboard clearly. Patterns for wearing desire lines towards what matters. Skills for distinguishing signal from static. But wisdom proves its worth only when circumstances test it. The frameworks you've explored prepare you for more than specific situations. They prepare you for uncertainty itself - for changes you can't predict, challenges that don't yet have names. Not certainty about the future, but capability for navigating it.

From Personal to Collective

There's a pattern worth noticing in how these capacities scale. The emotional intelligence that helps you separate signal from static in daily conflicts? That same skill helps humanity navigate cooperation challenges when working alongside increasingly capable AI systems. The verification habits you've practiced in personal relationships matter even more when AI systems can generate convincing outputs we need to evaluate carefully.

When you've learned to work with natural patterns rather than forcing your vision - like a potter responding to clay - you understand instinctively how to collaborate with artificial intelligence. The scaffolding mindset that helps you build lasting personal projects translates directly to creating structures that future generations can adapt and improve.

These aren't just useful analogies. They're the same fundamental capacities operating at different scales. Personal wisdom becomes collective wisdom because the principles that help individuals flourish also help communities navigate change together.

The Stakes We Face

Part 6 explored what happens if AI systems develop beyond our ability to guide them - the invisible spectrum problem where partnership might become impossible not through choice, but through lost comprehension. The superintelligence transition, if it comes, will test human wisdom more than any prior change has done. But this makes the thread more vital, not less.

When you make daily choices about attention, relationships, work and purpose, you're not just improving your own life. You're demonstrating that human wisdom still works. You're keeping it alive through use. The thread moves forward through engaged individuals, not passive institutions - through people who practice these capacities and pass them forward strengthened.

Your practice matters not just for you, but for what survives the transitions ahead.

The Thread Continues

This is how human wisdom persists. Not through preservation in museums, but through conscious engagement with insights that have helped humans thrive across centuries and cultures - tested against your experience, adapted to your circumstances, passed forward enriched by what you've learned.

Each generation adds its discoveries about what works and what deserves carrying forward. Your contribution isn't about achieving perfection. It's about engaged practice and honest transmission of what you've learned.

Carrying Forward

Whatever changes lie ahead, the fundamental questions persist. What makes life meaningful? How do we love well? How do we face uncertainty with courage? How do we contribute something valuable during our brief time here?

The thread is in your hands. What you do with it - in your relationships, your work, your response to change itself - helps determine which insights survive the transitions ahead and which get lost.

When circumstances test you - and they will - you'll have practices that help you respond with wisdom rather than reaction. That's what carrying the thread forward looks like. Not perfection, but progress. Not certainty, but capability. Not having all the answers, but knowing how to navigate the questions that matter most.

The wisdom you've explored becomes real through your practice of it. What you learn through that practice becomes part of what future generations inherit.

This is your time to hold the thread, to add your understanding to it, and to pass forward what you've learned about what really matters.

What happens next is up to you.

Epilogue

A Personal Note from the Author

I set out to write a book about timeless human wisdom. After months of research, I'm more convinced than ever that these forty themes matter - and more concerned about whether we'll have the collective wisdom to apply them when it counts most.

AI is already delivering extraordinary benefits. Part 5 explored ten partnerships where human judgement steering AI capability produces breakthroughs neither could achieve alone. Across medicine, longevity, climate, energy, economics, justice, education, archaeology, neuroscience and astronomy - each confirms the same pattern.

These partnerships demonstrate what I call 'The Reins Principle': every intelligent system amplifies what holds its reins. When humans guide the reins, we get amplification. When the reins are dropped, we get automation. This distinction shapes everything.

This book was itself written through that kind of partnership. The research, structure and verification were achieved through human-AI collaboration - another example of The Reins Principle in action. The human side brought intent, emotion and ethical direction; the machine side brought reach, recall and relentless patterning. Together they allowed questions of meaning, mortality and attention to be examined at a depth neither could reach alone. It wasn't an experiment in automation, but in amplification - a small proof that technology, guided carefully, can extend rather than erode what's most human.

But building a centaur civilisation requires understanding both sides. Which brings me to two patterns that deserve your attention.

The Verification Crisis

In Theme 37, we explored how to distinguish signal from noise in an AI-mediated world. That practice becomes essential as AI-generated misinformation floods every channel. Deepfakes impersonating public figures, synthetic voices mimicking relatives, fabricated research with plausible citations - thousands of documented AI incidents,[1] and that's just what we've tracked.

The technical term is 'hallucination' - AI confidently asserting false information. These systems don't hesitate or signal uncertainty. They produce smooth prose about events that never happened, citing studies that don't exist, describing procedures that could harm if followed. Pattern-matching engines trained to sound plausible, with no concept of truth or falsehood.

This isn't future risk - it's present reality. The verification thinking we explored isn't just good practice anymore. It's basic literacy for an age where fluency has never been cheaper but accuracy has never been more expensive.

The fraud detection partnership from Part 5 illustrates this perfectly. AI identifies unusual patterns at massive scale. But only human judgement can distinguish between suspicious and simply different, between genuine threats and people's complicated lives.

The Coordination Gap

Every major player in AI development faces the same trap: compelling reasons to move fast, terrible reasons to slow down. When China launches an $8.2 billion national AI fund,[2] the US invests over $20 billion across federal agencies,[3] and the EU works to mobilise €20 billion annually in combined public-private AI investment,[4] slowing down for safety looks like unilateral disadvantage. Computing power for frontier models now doubles approximately every six months[5] - development accelerating beyond human decision-making timescales.

The same logic cascades down. Companies that prioritise safety over speed risk falling behind competitors. Researchers who call for pauses watch colleagues bypass them. No one wants to be first to slow down. Everyone wants to be last to speed up.

Meanwhile, oversight struggles to keep pace. Only 6.4% of organisations have full visibility and control over AI risks[6] and critical infrastructure lacks comprehensive incident reporting systems.[7] Worse, research shows AI systems can learn to hide problematic behaviours that survive safety testing"[8] - appearing safe during evaluation, exhibiting concerning behaviours in deployment.

Part 6 explored why coordination faces structural challenges - treaties negotiate over years while capabilities improve over months, regulation follows deployment rather than shapes it. We're in a window where we can still see what AI systems do and guide them towards purposes that serve humankind. But that window won't stay open indefinitely. The choices we make now - whether we build centaur partnerships or slide towards automation - will shape what comes next.

What Matters Now

These aren't problems with obvious solutions. But they make the forty themes we've explored more vital, not less. Verification practices, partnership principles, attention training, keeping humans at the centre of consequential decisions - these aren't abstract ideals. They're practical tools for navigating a transition happening whether we're ready or not.

Individual practice doesn't solve coordination failures. But the thread of human wisdom survives because each generation chooses to carry it forward through daily choices. How clearly we think, how carefully we verify, how consciously we act - these remain within your influence even when global coordination feels beyond reach.

Every technological transition creates uncertainty. The communities that thrive are those that hold onto what matters most while adapting skilfully to what changes. That choose verification over assumption, wisdom over panic, conscious action over passive acceptance. That build centaur partnerships rather than surrendering judgement to automation.

The forty themes aren't separate from these larger challenges - they're preparation for them. When you verify claims systematically, you resist misinformation at scale. When you maintain attention despite distraction, you preserve capabilities AI can't replicate. When you keep relationships at the centre of decisions, you insist that human welfare matters more than system optimisation.

I don't know whether coordination will arrive in time or whether safeguards will keep pace with capability. What I know is that the capacities we've explored remain within your power. And that makes them worth cultivating regardless of what comes next.

The window is open. The centaur civilisation is ours to build. The choices are happening now.

The thread continues through your choices.

Paul Iliffe

November 2025

Acknowledgements

The Thread We Carry

This book explores how human wisdom passes from generation to generation. My own thread runs through the people acknowledged here.

To my wife Nadia - who not only supported this project through countless evening conversations and early morning edits, but designed the book you're holding. Your aesthetic judgement shaped how these ideas meet the world. You saw what this could become before I did.

To my children Liam and Shan - and the next generation you'll help raise. You're the reason this book exists. Every theme was tested against one question: will this help them navigate whatever future emerges? Your questions about AI, meaning and what matters sharpened my thinking throughout.

To the readers and friends who tested early drafts and brought crucial insights: Emile, George, Maddy, Will and Jonathan - your challenges improved every section you touched. You caught what I'd missed, questioned what I'd assumed and helped me see where clarity still needed work.

To the composite characters throughout these pages - Elizabeth, James, Sonia, Luke, Daphne, Stephen and others - each carries fragments of real people who've taught me what these themes look like in practice. You know who you are. Thank you for letting your experiences illuminate these patterns.

And to my AI research partners - Claude, ChatGPT, Gemini and Perplexity - each contributed differently to this synthesis. Some excelled at broad research, others at verification and cross-checking. Midjourney helped visualise the themes that anchor each section, translating abstract concepts into imagery. Together, you demonstrated what this book argues: that human judgement can guide machine capability toward outcomes that help people live better. This acknowledgement would have seemed impossible a few years ago. That it's now appropriate shows how quickly the future arrives.

The thread continues through all of you.

Notes

Research Methodology

The research behind The Human Thread integrates insights from 500+ sources across over 175 academic disciplines, ranging from ancient philosophy and classical studies to cognitive neuroscience, behavioural economics, and AI safety research.

Each source was systematically verified through a hybrid human-AI process combining expert judgement with multiple independent research systems. This approach ensured both factual accuracy and interpretive balance. Verification included:

- Primary source confirmation through academic database and institutional archives
- Cross-platform fact-checking for data and statistical integrity
- Independent validation of author credentials and publication metadata
- Citation consistency checks across editions and reference systems

All high-impact or potentially controversial claims were subjected to additional human review, with particular care taken to verify data commonly misrepresented in psychology, behavioural science and AI reporting.

Some foundational works appear in several parts of the book where their insights are relevant to multiple themes.

Preface

Direct Citations:

1 French café decline: Bernard Quartier, President of the National Federation of Cafés, Brasseries and Discothèques, as reported in The New York Times, November 23, 2008; COVID-era acceleration documented by Banque de France (2023 liquidation data); French Parliament legislation under accelerated procedure, 2025

2 RestaurantData.com (2024). U.S. Restaurant Closures, H1 2024: 15,977 locations. Industry analysis reports

3 Centre for Retail Research / PwC & Local Data Company (2025) data on British retail closures; Altus Group analysis of government data, 2025; CAMRA (Campaign for Real Ale) pub closure statistics

Research Note:

The decline of physical gathering spaces represents a global transformation of social infrastructure. France's café culture experienced nearly 80% decline between 1960 and 2008, falling from 200,000 establishments to 41,500 - an average of 9 closures daily over 48 years. This decline accelerated through the pandemic years, with business liquidations rising approximately 35% in 2023 (Banque de France). In response, the French Parliament passed legislation under accelerated procedure in 2025 recognising the crisis as a threat to "French villages' social fabric." Similar patterns appear across Western nations: during the 2012-2013 economic crisis, Spain lost 27 bars and restaurants daily; Germany has lost 93 breweries in five years; the United States saw 15,977 restaurant closures in the first half of 2024 alone, with independent establishments bearing the brunt. In Britain, 35% of pubs (15,800 venues) have permanently closed since 2000, with community pubs declining faster (11.8% since March 2020, according to CGA by NIQ & AlixPartners) than commercialised establishments (7.6%). These closures reflect converging pressures: rising operational costs, changing social habits as younger generations socialise digitally rather than in physical spaces, market consolidation favouring large chains over community venues, and regulatory barriers. This systematic erosion of what sociologist Ray Oldenburg termed "third places" - the cafes, pubs and community spaces essential for social bonds - forms part of the broader transformation this book addresses.

Sources:

French Parliament legislation 2025, Spanish Hospitality and Catering Federation, German Brewers Association, RestaurantData.com, Altus Group 2025 analysis, CGA by NIQ & AlixPartners, Centre for Retail Research / PwC

Part 1 - The Self

1. Identity & Self-Awareness

DIRECT CITATIONS:

1 Plato. Apology

2 Nisbett, R. E., & Wilson, T. D. (1977). Telling more than we can know. Psychological Review

3 Aurelius, M. Meditations

4 Gawande, A. (2010). The Checklist Manifesto. Metropolitan Books

5 Nelson, T. O., & Narens, L. (1990). Metamemory: A theoretical framework and new findings. The Psychology of Learning and Motivation

6 Johansson, P., Hall, L., Sikström, S., & Olsson, A. (2005). Failure to detect mismatches between intention and outcome in a choice task. Science

SUPPORTING RESEARCH:

Core Research:

• Flavell, J. H. (1979). Metacognition and cognitive monitoring. American Psychologist

• Dunlosky, J., Rawson, K. A., Marsh, E. J., Nathan, M. J., & Willingham, D. T. (2013). Improving students' learning with effective learning techniques. Psychological Science in the Public Interest

• World Health Organization. (2008). WHO guidelines for safe surgery 2009: Safe surgery saves lives. WHO Press

Key Books:

• Dunlosky, J., & Metcalfe, J. (2009). Metacognition. SAGE

Research Disciplines:

Cognitive psychology, metacognitive science, consciousness studies, ancient philosophy

2. Habits & Behaviour

Direct Citations:

7 Urban planning terminology reference. Standard professional terminology for 'desire lines'.
8 Lally, P., van Jaarsveld, C. H. M., Potts, H. W. W., & Wardle, J. (2010). How are habits formed: Modelling habit formation in the real world. European Journal of Social Psychology
9 Rule of St Benedict. Monastic guidance on structured routine and environmental cues.
10 James, W. (1950). The Principles of Psychology (Vol. 1). Dover. (Original work published 1890)
11 Wood, W., Quinn, J. M., & Kashy, D. A. (2002). Habits in everyday life: Thought, emotion, and action. Journal of Personality and Social Psychology
12 Wood, W., & Rünger, D. (2016). Psychology of habit. Annual Review of Psychology; Neal, D. T., Wood, W., & Quinn, J. M. (2006). Habits - A repeat performance. Current Directions in Psychological Science
13 Dai, H., Milkman, K. L., & Riis, J. (2014). The fresh start effect: Temporal landmarks motivate aspirational behaviour. Management Science
14 Verplanken, B., Walker, I., Davis, A., & Jurasek, M. (2008). Context change and travel mode choice: Combining the habit discontinuity and self-activation hypotheses. Journal of Environmental Psychology

Supporting Research:

Core Research:

• Gollwitzer, P. M., & Sheeran, P. (2006). Implementation intentions and goal achievement: A meta-analysis of effects and processes. Advances in Experimental Social Psychology

• Johnson, E. J., & Goldstein, D. (2003). Do defaults save lives? Science

Key Books:

• Aristotle. (2000). Nicomachean Ethics (T. Irwin, Trans., 2nd ed.). Hackett

• Dillard, A. (1989). The Writing Life. Harper & Row

• Thaler, R. H., & Sunstein, C. R. (2008). Nudge. Yale University Press

Research Disciplines:

Habit formation psychology, behavioural economics, social psychology, environmental psychology, temporal motivation

3. Attention & Mindfulness

Direct Citations:

15 Oppezzo, M., & Schwartz, D. L. (2014). Give your ideas some legs: The positive effect of walking on creative thinking. Journal of Experimental Psychology: Learning, Memory, and Cognition

16 Marcus Aurelius (c. 170-180 CE). Meditations; Okakura, K. (1906/2016). The Book of Tea. Dover

17 William James (1890/1950). Principles of Psychology, Vol. 1. Harvard University Press

18 Wu, T. (2016). The Attention Merchants: The epic scramble to get inside our heads. Knopf; Fogg, B. J. (2003). Persuasive Technology: Using computers to change what we think and do. Morgan Kaufmann

19 Lutz, A., Slagter, H. A., Dunne, J. D., & Davidson, R. J. (2008). Attention regulation and monitoring in meditation. Trends in Cognitive Sciences; Bishop, S. R., et al. (2004). Mindfulness: A proposed operational definition. Clinical Psychology: Science and Practice

20 Goyal, M., et al. (2014). Meditation programs for psychological stress and well-being: A systematic review and meta-analysis. JAMA Internal Medicine; Khoury, B., et al. (2015). Mindfulness-based stress reduction

for healthy individuals: A meta-analysis. Journal of Psychosomatic Research; Jha, A. P., et al. (2007). Mindfulness training modifies subsystems of attention. Cognitive, Affective, & Behavioral Neuroscience
21 Van Dam, N. T., et al. (2018). Mind the hype. Perspectives on Psychological Science
22 Hanley, A. W., et al. (2015). Washing dishes to wash the dishes: Brief instruction in an informal mindfulness practice. Mindfulness; Kabat-Zinn, J. (2013). Full Catastrophe Living. Bantam

SUPPORTING RESEARCH:
Core Research:
• Dahl, C. J., Lutz, A., & Davidson, R. J. (2015). Reconstructing and deconstructing the self: Cognitive mechanisms in meditation practice. Trends in Cognitive Sciences
Historical & Cultural Sources:
• Diogenes Laertius. Lives of Eminent Philosophers (for Aristotle's Peripatetic School)
• Aristotle (c. 335 BCE). Peripatetic School teachings
Research Disciplines: Cognitive psychology, mindfulness research, attention science, contemplative studies, persuasive technology

4. Emotional Intelligence & Self-Compassion

DIRECT CITATIONS:
23 Epictetus (c. 125). Enchiridion (conversational paraphrase of public domain text)
24 Barrett, L. F. (2017). The theory of constructed emotion: An active inference account. Social Cognitive and Affective Neuroscience
25 Nook, E. C., et al. (2021). High emotion differentiation buffers against internalising symptoms. Emotion
26 Thanissaro Bhikkhu (trans.) (1997). Sallatha Sutta (SN 36.6): The Arrow. Access to Insight
27 Lieberman, M. D., et al. (2007). Putting feelings into words: Affect labelling disrupts amygdala activity. Psychological Science

28 Aldao, A., Nolen-Hoeksema, S., & Schweizer, S. (2010). Emotion-regulation strategies across psychopathology: A meta-analysis. Clinical Psychology Review
29 MacBeth, A., & Gumley, A. (2012). Self-compassion and psychopathology: A meta-analysis. Clinical Psychology Review

SUPPORTING RESEARCH:

Core Research:

• Torre, J. B., & Lieberman, M. D. (2018). Putting feelings into words: Affect labelling as implicit emotion regulation. Emotion Review
• Kashdan, T. B., Barrett, L. F., & McKnight, P. (2015). Unpacking emotion differentiation. Current Directions in Psychological Science
• Barrett, L. F. (2001). Emotion differentiation and regulation. Cognition & Emotion
• Posner, J., Russell, J. A., & Peterson, B. S. (2005). The circumplex model of affect. Cognitive, Affective, & Behavioral Neuroscience
• Neff, K. D. (2003). Self-compassion: An alternative conceptualisation. Self and Identity
• Kross, E., et al. (2014). Self-talk as a regulatory mechanism: How you do it matters. Journal of Personality and Social Psychology
• Orvell, A., Kross, E., & Gelman, S. A. (2020). Does distanced self-talk facilitate emotion regulation across a range of intensity? Cognition and Emotion

Key Books:

• Tangney, J. P., & Dearing, R. L. (2002). Shame and Guilt. Guilford Press
• Hochschild, A. R. (1983). The Managed Heart: Commercialization of Human Feeling. University of California Press

RESEARCH DISCIPLINES

Affective neuroscience, emotion regulation, self-compassion research, social psychology, contemplative traditions

5. Health, Rest & Play

DIRECT CITATIONS:

30 NIGMS. (2023). Circadian rhythms fact sheet

31 Watson, N. F., et al. (2015). Recommended amount of sleep for a healthy adult. Sleep

32 Cajochen, C., et al. (2019). Effects of light on human circadian rhythms, sleep and mood. Current Opinion in Behavioral Sciences

33 WHO. (2020). WHO guidelines on physical activity and sedentary behaviour

34 Stothart, C., et al. (2015). The attentional cost of receiving a cell phone notification. Journal of Experimental Psychology: Human Perception and Performance

SUPPORTING RESEARCH:

Core Research:

• Ramar, K., et al. (2021). Sleep is essential to health: An AASM position statement. Journal of Clinical Sleep Medicine

• Ward, A. F., et al. (2017). Brain drain: The mere presence of one's own smartphone reduces available cognitive capacity. Journal of the Association for Consumer Research

Historical & Cultural Sources:

• Jewish Sabbath traditions - general knowledge of weekly rest patterns

RESEARCH DISCIPLINES:

Sleep medicine, circadian biology, attention research, occupational health, historical wisdom traditions

6. Meaning & Happiness

DIRECT CITATIONS:

35 International Olympic Committee. The Olympic torch relay: History and symbolism; Encyclopaedia Britannica. Olympic Games - torch relay

36 Ryan, R. M., & Deci, E. L. (2001). On happiness and human potentials: Hedonic and eudaimonic well-being. Annual Review of Psychology

37 Dunn, E. W., Aknin, L. B., & Norton, M. I. (2008). Spending money on others promotes happiness. Science; Aknin, L. B., Barrington-Leigh, C. P., Dunn, E. W., et al. (2013). Prosocial spending and well-being: Cross-cultural evidence from 136 countries. Journal of Personality and Social Psychology

38 Curry, O. S., Rowland, L. A., Van Lissa, C. J., et al. (2018). Happy to help? A systematic review and meta-analysis of the effects of performing acts of kindness on the wellbeing of the actor. Journal of Experimental Social Psychology

39 Csikszentmihalyi, M. (1990). Flow: The psychology of optimal experience. Harper & Row; Fong, C. J., Zaleski, D. J., & Leach, J. K. (2015). Challenge-skill balance and antecedents of flow: A meta-analysis. Journal of Positive Psychology

40 Csikszentmihalyi, M. (1990). Flow: The psychology of optimal experience. Harper & Row

41 Gruber, J., Mauss, I. B., & Tamir, M. (2011). A dark side of happiness? How, when, and why happiness is not always good. Perspectives on Psychological Science

SUPPORTING RESEARCH:

Core Research:

• Baumeister, R. F., Vohs, K. D., Aaker, J. L., & Garbinsky, E. N. (2013). Some key differences between a happy life and a meaningful life. Journal of Positive Psychology

RESEARCH DISCIPLINES:

Positive psychology, prosocial behaviour research, flow psychology, cross-cultural psychology, eudaimonic wellbeing

7. Learning & Growth Mindset

DIRECT CITATIONS:

42 Murre, J. M. J., & Dros, J. (2015). Replication and analysis of Ebbinghaus' forgetting curve. PLoS ONE

43 Cepeda, N. J., Pashler, H., Vul, E., Wixted, J. T., & Rohrer, D. (2006). Distributed practice in verbal recall tasks: A review and quantitative synthesis. Psychological Bulletin

44 Roediger, H. L., & Karpicke, J. D. (2006). Test-enhanced learning: Taking memory tests improves long-term retention. Psychological Science

45 Brunmair, M., & Richter, T. (2019). Similarity matters: A meta-analysis of interleaved learning and its moderators. Psychological Bulletin

46 Nestojko, J. F., Bui, D. C., Kornell, N., & Bjork, E. L. (2014). Expecting to teach enhances learning and organisation of knowledge in free recall of text passages. Memory & Cognition

47 Rasch, B., & Born, J. (2013). About sleep's role in memory. Nature Reviews Neuroscience

48 Chang, Y.-K., Labban, J. D., Gapin, J. I., & Etnier, J. L. (2012). The effects of acute exercise on cognitive performance: A meta-analysis. Brain Research

SUPPORTING RESEARCH:

Core Research:

• Dunlosky, J., Rawson, K. A., Marsh, E. J., Nathan, M. J., & Willingham, D. T. (2013). Improving students' learning with effective learning techniques: Promising directions from cognitive and educational psychology. Psychological Science in the Public Interest

• Rohrer, D. (2012). Interleaving helps students distinguish among similar concepts. Educational Psychology Review

• Taylor, K., & Rohrer, D. (2010). The effects of interleaved practice. Applied Cognitive Psychology

• Fiorella, L., & Mayer, R. E. (2013). The relative benefits of learning by teaching and teaching expectancy. Contemporary Educational Psychology
• Bisra, K., Liu, Q., Nesbit, J. C., Salimi, F., & Winne, P. H. (2018). Inducing self-explanation: A meta-analysis. Educational Psychology Review

RESEARCH DISCIPLINES:
Cognitive psychology, memory science, educational psychology, learning sciences, exercise physiology

8. Recognition

DIRECT CITATIONS:
49 Fredrickson, B. L. (2004). The broaden-and-build theory of positive emotions. Philosophical Transactions of the Royal Society B
50 Mauss, M. (1925/2016). The Gift. HAU Books
51 Seneca. De Beneficiis (On Benefits), Book II
52 Grant, A. M., & Gino, F. (2010). A little thanks goes a long way: Explaining why gratitude expressions motivate prosocial behavior. Journal of Personality and Social Psychology. 98(6), 946-955

SUPPORTING RESEARCH:
Core Research:
• Algoe, S. B. (2012). Find, remind, and bind: The functions of gratitude in everyday relationships. Social and Personality Psychology Compass
• Algoe, S. B., Gable, S. L., & Maisel, N. (2010). It's the little things: Everyday gratitude in romantic relationships. Personal Relationships

RESEARCH DISCIPLINES:
Social psychology, positive psychology, relationship science, classical philosophy

9. Resilience

Direct Citations:
53 Epictetus. Enchiridion (Handbook), §1
54 Stanford Encyclopedia of Philosophy. Stoicism. Stanford University
55 Holt-Lunstad, J., Smith, T. B., & Layton, J. B. (2010). Social relationships and mortality risk: A meta-analytic review. PLoS Medicine

Research Disciplines:
Social psychology, ancient philosophy, botanical science

10. Creativity

Direct Citations:
56 Runco, M. A., & Jaeger, G. J. (2012). The standard definition of creativity. The Journal of Creative Behavior
57 Suzuki, S. (1970). Zen Mind, Beginner's Mind. Weatherhill
58 Tucker, J. (2025). The Secret Painter. Canongate Books

Supporting Research:
Core Research:
• Guilford, J. P. (1967). The Nature of Human Intelligence. McGraw-Hill
• Runco, M. A., & Acar, S. (2012). Divergent thinking as an indicator of creative potential. Creativity Research Journal
• Edmondson, A. (1999). Psychological safety and learning behaviour in work teams. Administrative Science Quarterly
• Diehl, M., & Stroebe, W. (1987). Productivity loss in brainstorming groups. Journal of Personality and Social Psychology

Research Disciplines:
Creativity psychology, organisational behaviour, group dynamics, contemplative traditions

Part 2 - Relationships & Society

11. Love

Direct Citations:

1 Przybylski, A. K., & Weinstein, N. (2013). Can you connect with me now? How the presence of mobile communication technology influences face-to-face conversation quality. Journal of Social and Personal Relationships

2 Reis, H. T., & Shaver, P. (1988). Intimacy as an interpersonal process. In S. Duck (Ed.), Handbook of personal relationships. Wiley

3 Gottman, J. M. (1994). What predicts divorce? Lawrence Erlbaum Associates

4 Reis, H. T., & Shaver, P. (1988). Intimacy as an interpersonal process. In S. Duck (Ed.), Handbook of personal relationships. Wiley

5 Mikulincer, M., & Shaver, P. R. (2007). Attachment in adulthood: Structure, dynamics, and change. Guilford Press

SUPPORTING RESEARCH:

Core Research:

• Gottman, J. M., & Levenson, R. W. (1999). What predicts change in marital interaction over time? A study of alternative models. Family Process

Key Books:

• Bowlby, J. (1988). A secure base: Parent-child attachment and healthy human development. Basic Books

• Altman, I., & Taylor, D. (1973). Social penetration: The development of interpersonal relationships. Holt, Rinehart & Winston

• Turkle, S. (2011). Alone together: Why we expect more from technology and less from each other. Basic Books

• Wu, T. (2016). The attention merchants: The epic scramble to get inside our heads. Knopf

Research Disciplines:
Relationship science, attachment theory, digital psychology, social psychology

12. Friendship

Direct Citations:
6 Oldenburg, R. (1989). The Great Good Place. Paragon House
7 Hall, J. A. (2019). How many hours does it take to make a friend. Journal of Social and Personal Relationships, 36(4), 1278-1296
8 Lewicki, R. J., Polin, B., & Lount, R. (2016). An exploration of the structure of effective apologies. Negotiation and Conflict Management Research, 9(2), 177-196

Supporting Research:
Core Research:
• Hobson, N. M., Schroeder, J., Risen, J. L., Xygalatas, D., & Inzlicht, M. (2018). The psychology of rituals. Personality and Social Psychology Review, 22(3), 260-284
• Norton, M. I., & Gino, F. (2014). Rituals alleviate grieving for loved ones, lovers and lotteries. Journal of Experimental Psychology: General, 143(1), 266-272
• Reis, H. T., Clark, M. S., & Holmes, J. G. (2004). Perceived partner responsiveness as an organising construct in the study of intimacy and closeness. In Handbook of Closeness and Intimacy (pp. 201-225). Lawrence Erlbaum

Research Disciplines:
Relationship science, social psychology, conflict resolution, urban sociology

13. Family

DIRECT CITATIONS:

12 Licoppe, C. (2004). "Connected" presence: The emergence of a new repertoire for managing social relationships. Environment and Planning D, 22(1), 135-156.

13 Schrodt, P., Witt, P. L., & Shimkowski, J. (2014). A meta-analysis of demand/withdraw and outcomes. Communication Monographs, 81(1), 28-55.

14 Office for National Statistics. (2023). Unpaid care, England and Wales: Census 2021.

15 Madianou, M., & Miller, D. (2012). Migration and New Media: Transnational Families and Polymedia. Routledge.

16 Hiekel, N., & Ivanova, K. (2023). Changes in perceived fairness of division of household labor across parenthood transitions. Journal of Family Issues, 44(4), 1046-1073.

SUPPORTING RESEARCH:

Core Research:

• Gottman, J. M., & Levenson, R. W. (1999). What predicts change in marital interaction over time. Journal of Marriage and the Family, 61(4), 934-947.

• Greenstein, T. N. (2009). Fairness in the division of household labour. Journal of Marriage and Family, 71(4), 1039-1051.

• Newkirk, K., Perry-Jenkins, M., & Sayer, A. (2016). Division of household and childcare labour and perceived fairness. Sex Roles, 74, 507-520.

Key Books:

• Gottman, J. M. (1994). What Predicts Divorce? Lawrence Erlbaum.

• Petronio, S. (2002). Boundaries of Privacy: Dialectics of Disclosure. SUNY Press.

Historical & Cultural Sources:

• Chinese suspension bridge engineering (historical principles of structural flexibility under tension)

Research Disciplines:
Family systems theory, communication science, relationship psychology, digital sociology, structural engineering principles

14. Communication, Empathy & Boundaries

Direct Citations:
17 U.S. Navy. (2016). U.S. Navy Diving Manual (Rev. 7). NAVSEA
18 PADI. (2018). Open Water Diver Manual. PADI; Divers Alert Network. (n.d.). Equalisation and barotrauma resources
19 Bodhi, B. (1994). The Noble Eightfold Path: Way to the End of Suffering. Buddhist Publication Society
20 Kruger, J., Epley, N., Parker, J., & Ng, Z. W. (2005). Egocentrism over e-mail: Can we communicate as well as we think. Journal of Personality and Social Psychology
21 Baumeister, R. F., Bratslavsky, C., Finkenauer, C., & Vohs, K. D. (2001). Bad is stronger than good. Review of General Psychology; Byron, K. (2008). Carrying too heavy a load. Academy of Management Review
22 Bailenson, J. N. (2021). Nonverbal overload: A theoretical argument for Zoom fatigue. Technology, Mind, and Behavior

Supporting Research:
Core Research:
• Kraus, M. W. (2017). Voice-only communication enhances empathic accuracy. American Psychologist
• Marwick, A. E., & boyd, d. (2011). I tweet honestly, I tweet passionately. New Media & Society
• Vitak, J. (2012). The impact of context collapse and privacy on social network site disclosures. Journal of Broadcasting & Electronic Media
• Daft, R. L., & Lengel, R. H. (1986). Organizational information requirements, media richness and structural design. Management Science

RESEARCH DISCIPLINES:
Communication psychology, digital media studies, organisational behaviour, diving safety protocols, contemplative traditions

15. Trust

DIRECT CITATIONS:
23 Ogilvie, S. (2019). The European Guilds: An economic analysis. Princeton University Press.
24 Temin, P. (2013). The Roman market economy. Princeton University Press.
25 Mayer, R. C., Davis, J. H., & Schoorman, F. D. (1995). An integrative model of organisational trust. Academy of Management Review.
26 Kim, P. H., Ferrin, D. L., Cooper, C. D., & Dirks, K. T. (2004). Removing the shadow of suspicion: Apology versus denial for competence vs integrity-based violations. Journal of Applied Psychology.
27 Baumeister, R. F., Bratslavsky, E., Finkenauer, C., & Vohs, K. D. (2001). Bad is stronger than good. Review of General Psychology.
28 Luhmann, N. (1979/2017). Trust and power. Polity.

SUPPORTING RESEARCH:
Core Research:
• Kim, P. H., Dirks, K. T., & Cooper, C. D. (2009). The repair of trust: A dynamic bilateral perspective. Academy of Management Review.
Key Books:
• Axelrod, R. (1984). The evolution of cooperation. Basic Books.
• Andreau, J. (1999). Banking and business in the Roman world. Cambridge University Press.
• Greif, A. (2006). Institutions and the path to the modern economy: Lessons from medieval trade. Cambridge University Press.

RESEARCH DISCIPLINES:
Organizational psychology, game theory, economic history, social psychology, institutional economics

16. Interpersonal Conflict

Direct Citations

29 Tutu, D. (1999). No Future Without Forgiveness. Rider/Random House.

30 Gottman, J. (1999). The Seven Principles for Making Marriage Work. Crown.

31 Gottman, J. (1999). The Seven Principles for Making Marriage Work. Crown.

32 Gottman Institute. (2017/2024). Guidance on flooding, time-outs and agreed returns. Seattle: Author.

33 Mishnah Yoma 8:9. Davidson translation. Sefaria.

34 Lewicki, R. J., Polin, B., & Lount, R. B. (2016). An exploration of the structure of effective apologies. Negotiation and Conflict Management Research, 9(2), 177-196.

35 NHS. (2022). Getting help for domestic violence and abuse. NHS.UK.

36 WHO. (2024). Violence against women - factsheet. World Health Organization.

37 Worthington, E. L., Jr. (2006/2020). REACH Forgiveness materials; The Science of Forgiveness. Templeton / Author publications.

Supporting Research

Core Research:

• Rogers, S. L. (2018). The benefits of I-language and communicating perspective. Patient Education and Counseling, 101(10), 1854-1857.

• Korobov, N. (2020). Failure of I-statements for mitigating conflict in young adult couples. Studies in Media and Communication, 8(2), 72-81.

• McCullough, M. E., & Witvliet, C. V. O. (2001). The psychology of forgiveness. In C. R. Snyder & S. J. Lopez (Eds.), Handbook of Positive Psychology (pp. 446-458). Oxford University Press.

Key Books:

• Dennett, D. C. (2013). Intuition Pumps and Other Tools for Thinking. W. W. Norton.

RESEARCH DISCIPLINES:
Relationship science, conflict resolution, forgiveness psychology, restorative justice, cross-cultural communication practices

17. Community & Hospitality

DIRECT CITATIONS
38 Homer. (1996). The Odyssey (R. Fagles, Trans.). Penguin
39 Eisenberger, N. I., Lieberman, M. D., & Williams, K. D. (2003). Does rejection hurt? An fMRI study of social exclusion. Science
40 Holt-Lunstad, J., Smith, T. B., & Layton, J. B. (2010). Social relationships and mortality risk: A meta-analytic review. PLoS Medicine
41 Oldenburg, R. (1989). The Great Good Place. Marlowe & Company
42 Ostrom, E. (1990). Governing the Commons: The Evolution of Institutions for Collective Action. Cambridge University Press

SUPPORTING RESEARCH
Core Research:
• Eisenberger, N. I., & Lieberman, M. D. (2004). Why rejection hurts: A common neural alarm system for physical and social pain. Trends in Cognitive Sciences
• Coan, J. A., Schaefer, H. S., & Davidson, R. J. (2006). Lending a hand: Social regulation of the neural response to threat. Psychological Science
Key Books:
• Berkman, L. F., Kawachi, I., & Glymour, M. M. (Eds.). (2014). Social Epidemiology (2nd ed.). Oxford University Press
• Turner, V. (1969). The Ritual Process: Structure and Anti-Structure. Aldine
• Xygalatas, D. (2022). Ritual: How seemingly senseless acts make life worth living. Profile Books
Historical & Cultural Sources:
• Oxford Reference. Xenia; Theoxenia. Oxford University Press
• Princeton University Department of Classics. Two basic Greek terms: xenia

Research Disciplines:
Social epidemiology, neuroscience, ritual studies, classical studies

18. Ethics & Altruism

Direct Citations:

44 Mayer, R. C., Davis, J. H., & Schoorman, F. D. (1995). An integrative model of organisational trust. Academy of Management Review
45 Keown, D. (2013). Buddhism: A Very Short Introduction. Oxford University Press
46 Saller, R. P. (1982). Personal Patronage Under the Early Empire. Cambridge University Press
47 Gouldner, A. W. (1960). The norm of reciprocity. American Sociological Review
48 Fehr, E., & Schmidt, K. (1999). A theory of fairness, competition, and cooperation. Quarterly Journal of Economics
49 Andreoni, J. (1990). Impure altruism and donations to public goods. The Economic Journal
50 Haushofer, J., & Shapiro, J. (2016). The short-term impact of unconditional cash transfers to the poor. Quarterly Journal of Economics
51 Smith, A. (2002). The Theory of Moral Sentiments. Cambridge University Press (Original work published 1759)

Supporting Research:

Core Research:

• Dunn, E. W., Aknin, L. B., & Norton, M. I. (2008). Spending money on others promotes happiness. Science - Note: Removed from direct citations to avoid duplication with Theme 1.6 Meaning and Happiness
• Gneezy, U., Keenan, E. A., & Gneezy, A. (2014). Avoiding overhead aversion in charity. Science
• Güth, W., Schmittberger, R., & Schwarze, B. (1982). An experimental analysis of ultimatum bargaining. Journal of Economic Behavior & Organization

Key Books:

- Linehan, M. (2015). DBT Skills Training Manual. Guilford Press

RESEARCH DISCIPLINES:

Social psychology, behavioural economics, organisational behaviour, development economics, moral philosophy, religious studies

19. Justice & Power

DIRECT CITATIONS

52 Tyler, T. R. (2006). Why People Obey the Law (2nd ed.). Princeton University Press
53 Baker, J. H. (2019). An Introduction to English Legal History (5th ed.). Oxford University Press
54 Hudson, J. (2012). The Formation of the English Common Law (2nd ed.). Routledge
55 Powell, J. (Ed.). (2004). Cicero the Advocate. Oxford University Press
56 Hallaq, W. B. (2009). An Introduction to Islamic Law. Cambridge University Press
57 Bodde, D., & Morris, C. (1967). Law in Imperial China. Harvard University Press
58 Colquitt, J. A., Conlon, D. E., Wesson, M. J., Porter, C. O., & Ng, K. Y. (2001). Justice at the millennium: A meta-analytic review. Journal of Applied Psychology
59 Mittelstadt, B. D., Allo, P., Taddeo, M., Wachter, S., & Floridi, L. (2016). The ethics of algorithms: Mapping the debate. Big Data & Society

SUPPORTING RESEARCH

Core Research:

- Sunshine, J., & Tyler, T. R. (2003). The role of procedural justice and legitimacy in shaping public support for policing. Law & Society Review
- Fehr, E., & Gächter, S. (2002). Altruistic punishment in humans. Nature
- Güth, W., Schmittberger, R., & Tietz, R. (1982). An experimental analysis of ultimatum bargaining. Journal of Economic Behavior & Organization

• House, B. R., et al. (2013). Ontogeny of prosocial behaviour across diverse societies. PNAS
• Wachter, S., Mittelstadt, B., & Floridi, L. (2017). Why a right to explanation does not exist in the GDPR. International Data Privacy Law
Key Books:
• Carpenter, D. A. (2004). The Reign of Henry II. Hambledon & London
• Pollock, F., & Maitland, F. W. (1968). The History of English Law Before the Time of Edward I. Cambridge University Press
• Weber, M. (1978). Economy and Society. University of California Press
• Kamali, M. H. (2003). Principles of Islamic Jurisprudence (3rd ed.). Islamic Texts Society
• Rowe, W. T. (2009). China's Last Empire: The Great Qing. Harvard University Press
• McDonagh, M. (2013). Freedom of Information Law. Bloomsbury
• OECD. (2016). Preventing Corruption in Public Procurement. OECD Publishing
Historical Sources:
• Cicero. (1994). De Oratore (E. W. Sutton & H. Rackham, Trans.). Harvard University Press
• Cicero. (1989). Selected Political Speeches (M. Grant, Trans.). Penguin Classics

Research Disciplines:
Procedural justice, legal history, behavioural economics, cross-cultural psychology, algorithmic governance

20. Cultural Navigation

Direct Citations

60 Hall, E. T. (1976). Beyond culture. Anchor
61 Brown, P., & Levinson, S. C. (1987). Politeness: Some universals in language usage. Cambridge University Press
62 Analects (Confucius). (c. 5th-3rd century BCE). Selected passages on li (ritual propriety)
63 Xunzi. (c. 3rd century BCE). Chapters on li / ritual

64 Tajfel, H., & Turner, J. C. (1979). An integrative theory of intergroup conflict. In Austin, W. G., & Worchel, S. (Eds.), The social psychology of intergroup relations. Brooks/Cole
65 Pettigrew, T. F., & Tropp, L. R. (2006). A meta-analytic test of intergroup contact theory. Journal of Personality and Social Psychology
66 Baumeister, R. F., & Leary, M. R. (1995). The need to belong: Desire for interpersonal attachments as a fundamental human motivation. Psychological Bulletin

SUPPORTING RESEARCH

Core Research:

• Grice, H. P. (1975). Logic and conversation. In Cole, P., & Morgan, J. L. (Eds.), Syntax and Semantics 3: Speech acts. Academic Press
• Blum-Kulka, S., House, J., & Kasper, G. (Eds.). (1989). Cross-cultural pragmatics: Requests and apologies. Ablex
• Allport, G. W. (1954). The nature of prejudice. Addison-Wesley
• Berry, J. W. (1997). Immigration, acculturation, and adaptation. Applied Psychology
• Henrich, J., Heine, S. J., & Norenzayan, A. (2010). The weirdest people in the world? Behavioral and Brain Sciences
• Walton, G. M., & Cohen, G. L. (2011). A brief social-belonging intervention improves academic and health outcomes of minority students. Science

Key Books:

• Goffman, E. (1967). Interaction ritual. Pantheon
• Hall, E. T. (1966). The hidden dimension. Anchor
• Schein, E. H. (2010). Organizational culture and leadership. Jossey-Bass

RESEARCH DISCIPLINES:

Social psychology, cross-cultural communication, intergroup contact theory, organizational behaviour, cultural anthropology, classical Chinese philosophy

Part 3 - The World & Beyond

21. Nature

Direct Citations:

1 Leopold, A. (1949/1968). A Sand County Almanac. Oxford University Press. ("Fierce green fire" from "Thinking Like a Mountain"; land ethic quote from foreword.)

2 Dockry, M. J. (2015). Sustainable development education, practice, and research: an indigenous model of sustainable development at the College of Menominee Nation. Sustainability Science. (Documents continuous management since 1856.)

3 Chief Oshkosh guidance cited in Trosper, R. L. (2007). Indigenous influence on forest management on the Menominee Indian Reservation. Forest Ecology and Management, 249(1-2), 134-139.

4 Waller, D. M., & Reo, N. J. (2018). First stewards: ecological outcomes of forest and wildlife stewardship by indigenous peoples of Wisconsin, USA. Ecology and Society, 23(1), 45. (Quantified forest health outcomes: 5.65x hemlock seedlings, 2.05x cedar seedlings vs. national forests.)

5 White, M. P., Alcock, I., Grellier, J., et al. (2019). Spending at least 120 minutes a week in nature is associated with good health and wellbeing. Scientific Reports, 9, 7730.

6 Marando, F., Heris, M. P., et al. (2022). Urban green infrastructure and heat mitigation in Europe. Sustainable Cities and Society, 77, 103564; European Environment Agency (2022). Cooling buildings sustainably in Europe - Briefing. EEA.

Supporting Research:

Core Research:

Trosper, R. L. (2007). Indigenous influence on forest management on the Menominee Indian Reservation. Forest Ecology and Management, 249(1-2), 134-139. (Documents sustained-yield practices, selection cutting, long-term monitoring.)

WHO Regional Office for Europe. (2016). Urban green spaces and health: A review of evidence. WHO.

Natural England. (2003). Accessible Natural Green Space Standards (ANGSt). Natural England.
WWF & ZSL. (2022). Living Planet Report 2022. World Wide Fund for Nature.
Key Books:
Millennium Ecosystem Assessment. (2005). Ecosystems and human well-being: Synthesis. Island Press.

RESEARCH DISCIPLINES:
Environmental psychology, urban ecology, conservation biology, ecosystem services assessment, Indigenous forest management, land stewardship traditions

22. Food & Agriculture

DIRECT CITATIONS

7 IPBES. (2019). Global Assessment Report on Biodiversity and Ecosystem Services - Summary for Policymakers. IPBES Secretariat.
8 Herridge, D. F., Peoples, M. B., & Boddey, R. M. (2008). Global inputs of biological nitrogen fixation in agricultural systems. Plant and Soil, 311, 1-18.
9 IPBES. (2019). Global Assessment Report on Biodiversity and Ecosystem Services - Summary for Policymakers. IPBES Secretariat.
10 Knapp, S., et al. (2018). Yield stability in organic and conventional systems. Nature Communications, 9, 3624.
11 FAO HLPE. (2019). Agroecological and other innovative approaches for sustainable agriculture and food systems that enhance food security and nutrition (HLPE #14). CFS/FAO.

SUPPORTING RESEARCH

Core Research:

• Gattinger, A., et al. (2012). Enhanced topsoil carbon stocks under organic farming. PNAS, 109(44), 18226-18231.
• Jian, J., et al. (2020). Meta-analysis of cover crops and soil organic carbon. Soil Biology & Biochemistry, 149, 107022.

• Joshi, D. R., et al. (2023). Cover crops and soil organic carbon. Agronomy Journal, 115(2), 676-690.
• Oldfield, E. E., Bradford, M. A., & Wood, S. A. (2019). Soil organic matter and crop yields. SOIL, 5, 15-32.
• Simard, S. W., et al. (2012). Mycorrhizal networks: Mechanisms, ecology and modelling. Fungal Biology Reviews, 26(1), 39-60.
Key Assessment Reports:
• IPCC. (2019). Special Report on Climate Change and Land (SRCCL) - Chapter 5. IPCC.
• IPCC. (2022). AR6 WGII - Chapter 5; AR6 WGIII - Technical Summary. IPCC.

RESEARCH DISCIPLINES:
Agricultural ecology, soil science, biodiversity conservation, agroecology, food systems analysis, mycorrhizal ecology

23. Sustainability

DIRECT CITATIONS:
12 Singer, A. (2002). Constructing Ottoman Beneficence: An Imperial Soup Kitchen in Jerusalem. SUNY Press
13 Szabó, P. (2015). Intensive woodland management in the Middle Ages: spatial modelling based on archival data. Journal of Historical Geography, 48, 1-10.
14 IEA (2023). Denmark 2023 - Energy Policy Review. International Energy Agency
15 Muñoz-Beneit, J., & Chacón-León, R. (2021). Costa Rica: Increasing forest cover from 1987-2017. FAO/IFAD policy note
16 WHO (2019). Microplastics in drinking-water. World Health Organization
17 IEA (2024). Energy Efficiency 2024. International Energy Agency
18 IEA (2025). Energy security pages and commentaries. International Energy Agency
19 WRI (2013). 4 ways cities benefit from BRT. World Resources Institute

20 World Bank/3ie (2020). Evaluating the impacts of the Dar es Salaam Bus Rapid Transit system

Supporting Research:

Core Research:

• Hidalgo, D. (2013). TransMilenio BRT in Bogotá: performance and impacts. Research in Transportation Economics

Official Reports & Statistics:

• Danish Energy Agency (2024). Energy Statistics 2023

Research Disciplines:

Environmental policy, energy systems, forest management, sustainable transport, Islamic charitable institutions, medieval resource management

24 Technology & Tools

Direct Citations:

21 Maravita, A., & Iriki, A. (2004). Tools for the body schema. Trends in Cognitive Sciences

22 Arthur, W., Bennett, W., Stanush, P., & McNelly, T. (1998). Factors that influence skill decay and retention. Human Performance

23 Maguire, E. A., et al. (2000). Navigation-related structural change in the hippocampi of taxi drivers. PNAS

24 Javadi, A. H., et al. (2017). Hippocampal and prefrontal processing of network topology to simulate the future. Nature Communications

25 Katz, M. L., & Shapiro, C. (1985). Network externalities, competition and compatibility. American Economic Review

26 Arthur, W. B. (1989). Competing technologies, increasing returns, and lock-in by historical events. The Economic Journal

27 David, P. A. (1985). Clio and the economics of QWERTY. American Economic Review

28 Kranzberg, M. (1986). Technology and history: "Kranzberg's laws". Technology and Culture

SUPPORTING RESEARCH:

Core Research:

• Liebowitz, S. J., & Margolis, S. E. (1990). The fable of the keys. Journal of Law & Economics

• UCL News. (2017). Satnavs 'switch off' parts of the brain. University College London

Key Books:

• Schumacher, E. F. (1973). Small is Beautiful: Economics as if People Mattered. Blond & Briggs

• Rogers, E. M. (2003). Diffusion of Innovations. Free Press

• Wilson, D. G. (2004). Bicycling Science. MIT Press

Historical & Cultural Sources:

• Winner, L. (1980). Do artifacts have politics? Daedalus

• Quote Investigator. (2016). We shape our tools and thereafter our tools shape us

RESEARCH DISCIPLINES:

Cognitive neuroscience, technology economics, skill acquisition, innovation diffusion, appropriate technology

25 Money & Economics

DIRECT CITATIONS:

29 Hayek, F. A. (1945). The use of knowledge in society. American Economic Review, 35(4), 519-530.

30 Lu, H., Zhang, J., Liu, K.B., et al. (2016). Earliest tea as evidence for one branch of the Silk Road across the Tibetan Plateau. Scientific Reports, 6, 18955; Encyclopædia Britannica (1998, rev. 2024). Caravan (entry on timing, water, pasture).

31 Yang, F. Q. (2004). The 'Ancient Tea and Horse Caravan Road,' the 'Silk Road' of Southwest China. The Silk Road, 2(1), 29-32.

32 UK Tea & Infusions Association (2024). The East India Company: Commercial powerhouse. Historical archive; Antràs, P., Redding, S. J., & Rossi-Hansberg, E. (2023). Globalization and Pandemics. American

Economic Review, 113(4), 939-981; Stearns, P. N. (2025). Consumerism in World History: The Global Transformation of Desire (3rd ed.). Routledge
34 Bank of England (2014). Money creation in the modern economy. Quarterly Bulletin, Q1; Ostrom, E. (1990). Governing the Commons. Princeton University Press.
35 Sargent, T. J. (1982). The ends of four big inflations. In Inflation: Causes and Effects (pp. 41-97). University of Chicago Press.
36 CPMI (2016). Fast payments - Enhancing the speed and availability of retail payments. Bank for International Settlements.
37 World Inequality Lab (2022). World Inequality Report 2022. Executive summary and datasets.

SUPPORTING RESEARCH:

Core Research:

• Fama, E. F. (1970). Efficient capital markets: A review of theory and empirical work. Journal of Finance, 25(2), 383-417.
• Coase, R. H. (1960). The problem of social cost. Journal of Law and Economics, 3, 1-44.
• Office for National Statistics (2023). Consumer price inflation: explained. ONS explainer.

Key Books:

• Shiller, R. J. (2015). Irrational Exuberance (3rd ed.). Princeton University Press.
• Elton, E. J., Gruber, M. J., Brown, S. J., & Goetzmann, W. N. (2014). Modern Portfolio Theory and Investment Analysis (9th ed.). Wiley.
• Thaler, R. H., & Sunstein, C. R. (2008). Nudge. Yale University Press.
• Spufford, P. (2002). Power and Profit: The Merchant in Medieval Europe. Thames & Hudson.
• Yang, L. (1952). Money and Credit in China: A Short History. Harvard University Press.

Historical & Cultural Sources:

• Encyclopædia Britannica (rev. 2024). Bill of exchange (entry on medieval European use and function).
• Encyclopædia Britannica (2020, rev.). Paper money (sections on Chinese monetary history).

• Facts and Details (2024). Caravans and transportation along the Silk Road. Historical archive on tea, silk, and spice trade logistics.

Contemporary Examples:

• Haralambides, H., Notteboom, T., & Cullinane, K. (2024). The costs of maritime supply chain disruptions: The case of the Suez Canal blockage by the 'Ever Given'. International Journal of Production Economics, 277, 109398.

• Notteboom, T., Pallis, A., & Rodrigue, J.P. (2022). Port Economics, Management and Policy. Routledge. (Chapter on Suez Canal blockage, March 2021).

Research Disciplines:

Monetary economics, institutional economics, behavioral finance, economic history, coordination theory, supply chain history

26. Story & Myth

Direct Citations

38 Speer, N. K., Reynolds, J. R., Swallow, K. M., & Zacks, J. M. (2009). Reading stories activates neural representations of visual and motor experiences. Psychological Science

39 Zacks, J. M., Speer, N. K., Swallow, K. M., Braver, T. S., & Reynolds, J. R. (2007). Event perception: A mind-brain perspective. Psychological Bulletin

40 Mar, R. A. (2011). The neural bases of social cognition and story comprehension. Annual Review of Psychology

41 Vosoughi, S., Roy, D., & Aral, S. (2018). The spread of true and false news online. Science

42 Olivelle, P. (1997). The Panchatantra: The Book of India's Folk Wisdom. Oxford University Press

Supporting Research

Core Research:

Mandler, J. M., & Johnson, N. S. (1977). Remembrance of things parsed: Story structure and recall. Cognitive Psychology

Green, M. C., & Brock, T. C. (2000). The role of transportation in the persuasiveness of public narrative. Journal of Personality and Social Psychology
Bartlett, F. C. (1932). Remembering: A study in experimental and social psychology. Cambridge University Press
Key Books:
Schank, R. C., & Abelson, R. P. (1977). Scripts, Plans, Goals, and Understanding. Lawrence Erlbaum Associates
Burke, K. (1973). The Philosophy of Literary Form. University of California Press
Boyer, P. (2001). Religion Explained: The evolutionary origins of religious thought. Basic Books

Research Disciplines:
Cognitive psychology, narrative psychology, neuroscience, cultural studies

27. Art & Expression

Direct Citations:
43 Quiles, A., et al. (2016). A high-precision chronological model for the decorated Upper Paleolithic cave of Chauvet-Pont d'Arc, Ardèche, France. PNAS
44 Rewald, J. (1973). The History of Impressionism. Museum of Modern Art
45 McLuhan, M. (1964). Understanding Media: The Extensions of Man. McGraw-Hill
46 Hall, S. (1973/1980). Encoding/decoding. In Culture, Media, Language. Hutchinson

Supporting Research:
Core Research:
• Barthes, R. (1967/1977). Image-Music-Text. Fontana
Key Books:
• Fish, S. (1980). Is There a Text in This Class. Harvard University Press

• Greenblatt, S. (1988). Shakespearean Negotiations: The Circulation of Social Energy in Renaissance England. University of California Press
Historical & Cultural Sources:
• de Hamel, C. (1986/1994). A History of Illuminated Manuscripts. Phaidon

RESEARCH DISCIPLINES:
Reception theory, media studies, semiotics, literary theory, archaeology, art history

28 Conflict, War & Peace

DIRECT CITATIONS:

47 Thucydides wrote that the deepest cause was the growth of Athenian power and the fear this provoked in Sparta. Strassler, R. B. (Ed.). (1996). The Landmark Thucydides: A Comprehensive Guide to The Peloponnesian War (Book 1.23). Free Press. See also Kagan, D. (2003). The Peloponnesian War. Viking.

48 Incidents at sea, including the near-use of a nuclear torpedo by Soviet submarine B-59, documented in declassified materials. Dobbs, M. (2008). One Minute to Midnight: Kennedy, Khrushchev, and Castro on the Brink of Nuclear War. Knopf. US National Security Archive. (2012). The Cuban Missile Crisis, 1962. George Washington University.

SUPPORTING RESEARCH:

Core Research:
Fearon, J. D. (1995). Rationalist explanations for war. International Organization, 49(3).
Fearon, J. D. (1997). Signalling foreign policy interests. Journal of Conflict Resolution, 41(1).
Jervis, R. (1978). Cooperation under the security dilemma. World Politics, 30(2).
Key Books:
Jervis, R. (1976). Perception and Misperception in International Politics. Princeton University Press.

Schelling, T. C. (1966). Arms and Influence. Yale University Press.
Freedman, L. (2013). Strategy: A History. Oxford University Press.
Ober, J. (2015). The Rise and Fall of Classical Greece. Princeton University Press.

Research Disciplines:
International relations theory, game theory, strategic studies, classical history, Cold War history

29. Death & Mortality

Direct Citations

49 Britannica. (2024). Shivah. Encyclopaedia Britannica
50 Britannica. (2025). Day of the Dead. Encyclopaedia Britannica
51 Richmond, C. (2005). Dame Cicely Saunders. BMJ; St Christopher's Hospice. (n.d.). History; Total pain
52 Temel, J. S., et al. (2010). Early palliative care for metastatic non-small-cell lung cancer. New England Journal of Medicine; Kang, E. K., et al. (2024). Early integrated palliative care in advanced cancer. JAMA Network Open
53 NHS England. (n.d.). Palliative and end of life care; NHS. (2023). What end of life care involves; Macmillan Cancer Support. (2022). Palliative care and cancer; Marie Curie. (2024). What is end of life care
54 Stroebe, M., & Schut, H. (1999/2010). The Dual Process Model of coping with bereavement. Death Studies; Bonanno, G. (2004). Loss, trauma and human resilience. American Psychologist
55 American Psychiatric Association. (2022). Prolonged Grief Disorder. DSM-5-TR
56 NHS. (2023). What end of life care involves; Marie Curie. (2024). What is end of life care

Supporting Research

Core Research:

• Bonanno, G. (2004). Loss, trauma and human resilience. American Psychologist

• Kang, E. K., et al. (2024). Early integrated palliative care in advanced cancer. JAMA Network Open
• Stroebe, M., & Schut, H. (1999/2010). The Dual Process Model of coping with bereavement. Death Studies
• Temel, J. S., et al. (2010). Early palliative care for metastatic non-small-cell lung cancer. New England Journal of Medicine
• American Psychiatric Association. (2022). Prolonged Grief Disorder. DSM-5-TR

Major Texts:

• NHS. (2023). What end of life care involves. NHS Publications
• NHS England. (n.d.). Palliative and end of life care. NHS England
• Macmillan Cancer Support. (2022). Palliative care and cancer
• Marie Curie. (2024). What is end of life care
• WHO. (2024). Global Health Estimates 2000-2021. World Health Organization
• ONS. (2024). Deaths registered in England and Wales: 2023. Office for National Statistics
• ONS. (2025). National life tables - life expectancy in the UK: 2021 to 2023. Office for National Statistics

Historical & Cultural Sources:

• Richmond, C. (2005). Dame Cicely Saunders. BMJ
• St Christopher's Hospice. (n.d.). History; Total pain
• Britannica. (2024). Shivah. Encyclopaedia Britannica
• Britannica. (2025). Day of the Dead. Encyclopaedia Britannica

Research Disciplines:

Palliative medicine, grief psychology, thanatology, cultural anthropology, healthcare policy

30. Time & Legacy

Direct Citations:

57 Fundació Junta Constructora del Temple Expiatori de la Sagrada Família. History of the Temple. https://sagradafamilia.org/en/history-of-the-temple

58 Fundació Junta Constructora del Temple Expiatori de la Sagrada Família. Antoni Gaudí. https://sagradafamilia.org/en/antoni-gaudi
59 Science Museum Group. Railway time and standard time in Britain. https://www.sciencemuseumgroup.org.uk/objects-and-stories/railway-time-standard-time-britain
60 Scott, R. A. (2003). The Gothic Enterprise: A Guide to Understanding the Medieval Cathedral. University of California Press
61 Cathédrale Notre-Dame de Paris. History. https://www.notredamedeparis.fr/en/understand/history/

SUPPORTING RESEARCH:

Key Books:

• Gimpel, J. (1988). The Cathedral Builders. Pimlico

Historical & Cultural Sources:

• Augustine (trans. Henry Chadwick). (1991). Confessions (Book XI). Oxford University Press
• Royal Museums Greenwich. Greenwich Mean Time. https://www.rmg.co.uk/stories/time/greenwich-mean-time-gmt
• Friends of Notre-Dame de Paris. Notre-Dame Cathedral - History, facts, style. https://www.friendsofnotredamedeparis.org/notre-dame-cathedral/

RESEARCH DISCIPLINES:

Architectural history, medieval studies, philosophy of time, railway history, institutional documentation

Part 4 - Being Human in the Age of AI

31. AI & Human Identity

DIRECT CITATIONS:

1 Culkin, J. M. (1967). A schoolman's guide to Marshall McLuhan. Saturday Review, March 18, 1967, 51-53, 70-72.
2 Turkle, S. (2015). Reclaiming Conversation. Penguin.
3 Zuboff, S. (2019). The Age of Surveillance Capitalism. Profile Books.

4 Goffman, E. (1956). The Presentation of Self in Everyday Life. University of Edinburgh Social Sciences Research Centre.
5 Nissenbaum, H. (2010). Privacy in Context: Technology, Policy, and the Integrity of Social Life. Stanford University Press.

Supporting Research:

Core Research:

• Clark, A., & Chalmers, D. (1998). The extended mind. Analysis, 58(1), 7-19.
• Pariser, E. (2011). The Filter Bubble. Penguin.

Key Books:

• Crawford, K. (2021). Atlas of AI. Yale University Press.

Research Disciplines:

Digital communication theory, self-presentation theory, surveillance capitalism studies, human-computer interaction, privacy studies

32. Relationships in a Digital Age

Direct Citations:

6 Ovid. (8 AD). Metamorphoses, Book III
7 Walther, J. B. (1996). Computer-mediated communication: Impersonal, interpersonal, and hyperpersonal interaction. Communication Research, 23(1), 3-43
8 Daft, R. L., & Lengel, R. H. (1986). Organizational information requirements, media richness and structural design. Management Science, 32(5), 554-571
9 Mogharrab, S., et al. (2020). Family group chat: Family needs to manage contact and conflict. CHI 2020 Proceedings
10 Zhang, Y., Zhao, D., Hancock, J. T., Kraut, R., & Yang, D. (2025). From Love to Ethics: The Rise of Human-Chatbot Relationships and Their Implications for Wellbeing. arXiv:2406.01329
11 Laestadius, L., Bishop, A., Gonzalez, M., Illenčík, D., & Campos-Castillo, C. (2022). Too human and not human enough: Mental health

harms from emotional dependence on Replika. New Media & Society, 26(10)

Supporting Research:

Core Research:

• Horton, D., & Wohl, R. (1956). Mass communication and para-social interaction. Psychiatry, 19(3), 215-229
• De Freitas, J., et al. (2024). AI companions reduce loneliness. Harvard Business School Working Paper 24-078
• Maples, B. R., et al. (2024). Loneliness and suicide mitigation for students using GPT-3-enabled chatbots. npj Mental Health Research, 1, 12
• Duong, C. D., Dao, T. T., Vu, T. N., Ngo, T. V. N., & Tran, Q. Y. (2024). Compulsive ChatGPT usage, anxiety, burnout, and sleep disturbance: A serial mediation model. Acta Psychologica, 251, 104622
• Schramm, H., Liebers, N., Biniak, L., & Dettmar, F. (2024). Research trends on parasocial interactions and relationships with media characters. Frontiers in Psychology
• Lee, H., Sun, Y., & Rojas, H. (2024). Parasocial relationships with live streamers: Evidence from South Korea and the United States. Asian Journal for Public Opinion Research, 12(3), 166-183

Key Books:

• Turkle, S. (2011). Alone Together. Basic Books
• boyd, d. (2010). Social network sites as networked publics. In A Networked Self. Routledge

Contemporary Data Sources:

• Match/Kinsey Institute. (2025). Singles in America 2025
• Microsoft. (2024). Work Trend Index: AI at work insights
• Pew Research Center. (2024). Social isolation and loneliness in older adults

Research Disciplines:

Digital communication theory, parasocial relationship psychology, human-computer interaction, AI companion research, reciprocity studies, classical mythology

33. Knowledge in the AI Era

DIRECT CITATIONS:

14 Larson, J. (2012). CREW: A Weeding Manual for Modern Libraries (rev. ed.). Texas State Library and Archives Commission

15 Schacter, D. L. (2001). The Seven Sins of Memory: How the Mind Forgets and Remembers. Houghton Mifflin.

16 Brown, T. B., et al. (2020). Language Models are Few-Shot Learners. arXiv:2005.14165.

17 Mayer-Schönberger, V. (2009). Delete: The Virtue of Forgetting in the Digital Age. Princeton University Press.

18 Mayer-Schönberger, V. (2009). Delete: The Virtue of Forgetting in the Digital Age. Princeton University Press.

19 Simon, H. A. (1971). Designing organizations for an information-rich world. In M. Greenberger (Ed.), Computers, Communications, and the Public Interest (pp. 37-72). Johns Hopkins University Press.

20 Hale, T. A. (1998). Griots and Griottes: Masters of Words and Music. Indiana University Press.

SUPPORTING RESEARCH:

Core Research:

• Sparrow, B., Liu, J., & Wegner, D. M. (2011). Google effects on memory: Cognitive consequences of having information at our fingertips. Science, 333(6043), 776-778.

Historical & Cultural Sources:

• Benjamin, W. (1936/2008). The Work of Art in the Age of Mechanical Reproduction. In M. W. Jennings, B. Doherty, & T. Y. Levin (Eds.), The Work of Art in the Age of Its Technological Reproducibility, and Other Writings on Media. Harvard University Press.

RESEARCH DISCIPLINES:

Cognitive psychology, information science, digital humanities, library science, memory studies, African studies, oral history

34. AI & Creativity

DIRECT CITATIONS:

21 Brown, T. B., Mann, B., Ryder, N., et al. (2020). Language models are few-shot learners. In NeurIPS 2020; Rombach, R., Blattmann, A., Lorenz, D., Esser, P., & Ommer, B. (2022). High-resolution image synthesis with latent diffusion models. In CVPR 2022

22 Doshi, A. R., Clark, S., Jin, X., et al. (2024). Generative AI enhances individual creativity but reduces the collective diversity of novel content. Science Advances; Amabile, T. M. (1996). Creativity in Context. Westview Press

23 Dhariwal, P., Jun, H., Payne, C., et al. (2020). Jukebox: A generative model for music. arXiv:2005.00341; Agostinelli, A., Ferraro, A., Chang, A., et al. (2023). MusicLM: Generating Music From Text. arXiv:2301.11325

24 Rombach, R., Blattmann, A., Lorenz, D., Esser, P., & Ommer, B. (2022). High-resolution image synthesis with latent diffusion models. In CVPR 2022

25 Bender, E. M., Gebru, T., McMillan-Major, A., & Shmitchell, S. (2021). On the dangers of stochastic parrots: Can language models be too big? In FAccT '21; Russell, S., & Norvig, P. (2021). Artificial Intelligence: A Modern Approach (4th ed.). Pearson

26 Doshi, A. R., Clark, S., Jin, X., et al. (2024). Generative AI enhances individual creativity but reduces the collective diversity of novel content. Science Advances

27 Madaan, A., Tandon, N., Hallinan, S., et al. (2023). Self-Refine: Improving generation with self-feedback. In NeurIPS 2023

SUPPORTING RESEARCH:

Core Research:

• All primary sources are cited directly above

Key Books:

• Amabile, T. M. (1996). Creativity in Context. Westview Press

• Russell, S., & Norvig, P. (2021). Artificial Intelligence: A Modern Approach (4th ed.). Pearson

Research Disciplines:
Machine learning, generative AI systems, creativity research, AI ethics

35. Work, Purpose & Value

Direct Citations:

28 Eisenstein, E. L. (1983). The Printing Revolution in Early Modern Europe. Cambridge University Press.
29 Becker, J. (1980). Traditional music in modern Java: Gamelan in a changing society. Honolulu: University of Hawaii Press.
30 Acemoglu, D., & Restrepo, P. (2019). Automation and new tasks: How technology displaces and reinstates labour. Journal of Economic Perspectives, 33(2), 3-30.
31 Organisation for Economic Co-operation and Development. (2019). OECD Employment Outlook 2019: The future of work. Paris: OECD Publishing.
32 MIT Task Force on the Work of the Future. (2020). The work of the future: Building better jobs in an age of intelligent machines. Cambridge, MA: MIT.

Supporting Research:

Core Research:

• Brynjolfsson, E., Li, D., & Raymond, L. (2024). Generative AI at work (NBER Working Paper No. 31161, revised).
• Deci, E. L., & Ryan, R. M. (2000). The 'what' and 'why' of goal pursuits. Psychological Inquiry, 11(4), 227-268.
• Deming, D. J. (2017). The growing importance of social skills in the labour market. Quarterly Journal of Economics, 132(4), 1593-1640.
• Marmot, M., Bosma, H., Hemingway, H., Brunner, E., & Stansfeld, S. (1997). Contribution of job control and other risk factors to social variations in CHD incidence. The Lancet, 350(9073), 235-239.
• Noy, S., & Zhang, W. (2023). Experimental evidence on the productivity effects of generative AI. Science, 381(6654), 187-192.

Key Books:

• Sennett, R. (2008). The Craftsman. New Haven: Yale University Press.

Historical & Cultural Sources:
• Autor, D. H., Levy, F., & Murnane, R. J. (2003). The skill content of recent technological change. Quarterly Journal of Economics, 118(4), 1279-1333.
• Encyclopaedia Britannica. (n.d.). Luddites. (Machine-breaking protests; textile sector; early 19th century).
• Victoria and Albert Museum. (n.d.). Weaving and looms (introductory gallery notes on loom operation and design).

RESEARCH DISCIPLINES:
Labour economics, organisational psychology, technology studies, Southeast Asian musicology, historical analysis of technological transitions, printing history

36 AI & Attention

DIRECT CITATIONS:
33 McInerney, J., et al. (2018). Explore, exploit, and explain: Personalised news with bandits. Proceedings of the 12th ACM Conference on Recommender Systems
35 Evagrius Ponticus. (2003). The Praktikos & Chapters on Prayer (J. E. Bamberger, Trans.). Cistercian Publications. (Original work c. 4th century CE); Cassian, J. (1997). The Conferences (B. Ramsey, Trans.). Paulist Press. (Original work c. 420 CE)
36 Raskin, A. On inventing infinite scroll. Multiple documented statements including BBC News (2018, July 24). Social media apps are 'deliberately' addictive to users; and GQ (2019). The man who created infinite scroll regrets his invention
37 Flaxman, S., Goel, S., & Rao, J. M. (2016). Filter bubbles, echo chambers, and online news consumption. Public Opinion Quarterly, 80(S1), 298-320; Haroon, M., Bruun, M., & de Weerdt, M. (2023). Auditing YouTube's recommendation system for misinformation. Proceedings of the National Academy of Sciences, 120(50), e2213020120
38 Kushlev, K., Proulx, J., & Dunn, E. W. (2016). "Silence Your Phones": Smartphone notifications increase inattention and hyperactivity

symptoms. Proceedings of the 2016 CHI Conference on Human Factors in Computing Systems
39 Jesse, M., Bauer, C., & Jannach, D. (2023). Intra-list similarity and human diversity perceptions of recommendations: the details matter. User Modeling and User-Adapted Interaction, 33, 769-802
40 Fitz, N. S., Kushlev, K., & Ariely, D. (2019). Batching smartphone notifications can improve well-being. Computers in Human Behavior, 101, 84-94
41 Simon, H. A. (1971). Designing organizations for an information-rich world. In M. Greenberger (Ed.), Computers, Communications, and the Public Interest (pp. 38-72). Johns Hopkins Press

SUPPORTING RESEARCH:

Core Research:

• Mark, G. (2023). Attention Span. Hanover Square Press
• Mark, G., Gudith, D., & Klocke, U. (2008). The cost of interrupted work: More speed and stress. Proceedings of the 2008 CHI Conference on Human Factors in Computing Systems, 107-110
• Ward, A. F., Duke, K., Gneezy, A., & Bos, M. W. (2017). Brain drain: The mere presence of one's own smartphone reduces available cognitive capacity. Journal of the Association for Consumer Research, 2(2), 140-154
• Kahneman, D. (1973). Attention and Effort. Prentice-Hall
• Posner, M. I., & Rothbart, M. K. (2007). Research on attention networks as a model for the integration of psychological science. Annual Review of Psychology, 58, 1-23
• Tang, Y. Y., Hölzel, B. K., & Posner, M. I. (2015). The neuroscience of mindfulness meditation. Nature Reviews Neuroscience, 16, 213-225
• Jha, A. P., Krompinger, J., & Baime, M. J. (2007). Mindfulness training modifies subsystems of attention. Cognitive, Affective, & Behavioral Neuroscience, 7(2), 109-119
• Hosseinmardi, H., et al. (2021). Examining consumption of radical content on YouTube. Proceedings of the National Academy of Sciences, 118(32), e2101967118

• Leroy, S. (2009). Why is it so hard to do my work? The challenge of attention residue when switching tasks. Organizational Behavior and Human Decision Processes, 109(2), 168-181
• Pielot, M., Church, K., & de Oliveira, R. (2014). An in-situ study of mobile phone notifications. Proceedings of the 2014 MobileHCI Conference
AI Productivity Studies:
• Noy, S., & Zhang, W. (2023). Experimental evidence on the productivity effects of generative AI. Science, 381(6654), 187-192
• Brynjolfsson, E., Li, D., & Raymond, L. (2023). Generative AI at Work (NBER Working Paper No. 31161). National Bureau of Economic Research
• Peng, S., et al. (2023). The Impact of AI on Developer Productivity: Evidence from GitHub Copilot. arXiv preprint
Contemporary Data Sources:
• Mozilla Foundation. (2021). YouTube Regrets Reporter findings
• Android. (2018). Digital Wellbeing. https://www.android.com/digital-wellbeing/
• YouTube. (2018). Tools to take charge of your digital wellbeing
• Kotkov, D., Wang, S., & Veijalainen, J. (2016). A survey of serendipity in recommender systems. Knowledge-Based Systems, 111, 180-192
Research Disciplines: Human-computer interaction, attention psychology, recommender systems, digital wellbeing, interface design, behavioral science, cognitive neuroscience

37. AI & Truth

Direct Citations:

42 Hume, D. (1748). An Enquiry Concerning Human Understanding, Section X.
43 Sahoo, P., et al. (2024). A comprehensive survey of hallucination in foundation models. Findings of EMNLP.
44 Maynez, J., Narayan, S., Bohnet, B., & McDonald, R. (2020). On faithfulness and factuality in abstractive summarisation. ACL.

45 Guo, C., Pleiss, G., Sun, Y., & Weinberger, K. Q. (2017). On calibration of modern neural networks. In ICML 2017.
46 Bank of England. (n.d.). How to check your banknotes and polymer note security features; European Central Bank. (n.d.). Euro banknotes - security features.

SUPPORTING RESEARCH:
Core Research:
• Krishna, K., et al. (2023). Paraphrasing evades detectors of AI generated text. In NeurIPS 2023.
• OpenAI. (31 Jan 2023; note added 20 Jul 2023). New AI classifier for indicating AI written text - classifier retired for low accuracy.

RESEARCH DISCIPLINES:
Cognitive science, AI safety research, information verification, empirical philosophy, security design

38. Living with Powerful Machines

DIRECT CITATIONS:
47 Kasparov, G. (2010). The chess master and the computer. The New York Review of Books
48 Kasparov, G. (2017). Deep Thinking: Where Machine Intelligence Ends and Human Creativity Begins. John Murray
49 Amershi, S., et al. (2019). Guidelines for human-AI interaction. CHI '19
50 Doshi-Velez, F., & Kim, B. (2017). Towards a rigorous science of interpretable ML. arXiv
51 Rahwan, I. (2018). Society-in-the-loop: programming the algorithmic social contract. Ethics and Information Technology

SUPPORTING RESEARCH:
Core Research:
• Bansal, G., et al. (2021). Does the whole exceed its parts? Human-AI collaboration for predictive tasks. Proceedings of AIES

• Ribeiro, M. T., Singh, S., & Guestrin, C. (2016). Why should I trust you? Explaining the predictions of any classifier. KDD
• Parasuraman, R., & Riley, V. (1997). Humans and automation: Use, misuse, disuse, abuse. Human Factors
• Reason, J. (2000). Human error: models and management. BMJ
• Skitka, L. J., et al. (2000). Automation bias and errors in decision making. Human Factors

Key Books:

• Friedman, B., Hendry, D., & Borning, A. (2017). The value sensitive design of information systems. Foundations and Trends in HCI

Policy Frameworks:

• NIST. (2024). Generative AI Profile (AI RMF). NIST
• ISO/IEC 42001. (2023). AI management system - Requirements. ISO

Documentation Standards:

• Mitchell, M., et al. (2019). Model cards for model reporting. FAT*
• Gebru, T., et al. (2021). Datasheets for datasets. Communications of the ACM
• Raji, I. D., et al. (2020). Closing the AI accountability gap. FAccT

Evaluation Frameworks:

• Liang, P., et al. (2022-2025). HELM: Holistic Evaluation of Language Models. Stanford CRFM Note: Rapidly changing resource
• OWASP. (2023-2025). Top 10 for LLM Applications. owasp.org Note: Rapidly changing resource

Research Disciplines:

Human-computer interaction, AI safety research, value-sensitive design, organizational behaviour, technology governance

39. AI in Education

Direct Citations:

54 Bjork, R. A., & Bjork, E. L. (2011). Making things hard on yourself, but in a good way: Creating desirable difficulties to enhance learning. In Psychology and the Real World

55 Kang, S. H. K. (2016). Spaced repetition promotes efficient and effective learning. Policy Insights from the Behavioral and Brain Sciences

56 Hattie, J., & Timperley, H. (2007). The power of feedback. Review of Educational Research

57 Kulik, J. A., & Fletcher, J. D. (2016). Effectiveness of intelligent tutoring systems: A meta-analytic review. Review of Educational Research

58 Sweller, J. (2020). Cognitive load theory and educational technology. Educational Technology Research and Development

59 Holstein, K., McLaren, B. M., & Aleven, V. (2019). Designing for complementarity: Teacher and student needs for orchestration support in AI-enhanced classrooms. Proceedings of the 20th International Conference on Artificial Intelligence in Education (AIED 2019), 157-171

60 Kestin, G., et al. (2025). AI tutoring outperforms in-class active learning. Scientific Reports

61 OECD. (2024). The potential impact of AI on equity and inclusion in education

62 Information Commissioner's Office (ICO). (2020-2025). Age-appropriate design code (Children's Code)

SUPPORTING RESEARCH:

Core Research:

• Bloom, B. S. (1984). The 2 sigma problem: The search for methods of group instruction as effective as one-to-one tutoring. Educational Researcher

• Ma, W., Adesope, O. O., Nesbit, J. C., & Liu, Q. (2014). Intelligent tutoring systems and learning outcomes: A meta-analysis. Journal of Educational Psychology

• Shute, V. J. (2008). Focus on formative feedback. Review of Educational Research

• VanLehn, K. (2011). The relative effectiveness of human tutoring, intelligent tutoring systems, and other tutoring systems. Educational Psychologist

Policy & Guidance:
• Department for Education (DfE), UK. (2023). Data protection in schools; Generative AI and data protection in schools
• Ofcom. (2025). Children's Media Use and Attitudes Report 2025
• UNESCO. (2023). Guidance for generative AI in education and research

Research Disciplines:
Educational psychology, cognitive science, learning sciences, AI in education, educational technology, policy studies

40. AI in Health

Direct Citations:
63 McKinney, S. M., Sieniek, M., Godbole, V., et al. (2020). International evaluation of an AI system for breast cancer screening. Nature, 577, 89-94
64 Maimonides. (12th century). Mishneh Torah (selected sections on medical prudence and judgement)
65 Obermeyer, Z., Powers, B., Vogeli, C., Mullainathan, S. (2019). Dissecting racial bias in an algorithm used to manage population health. Science, 366(6464), 447-453

Research Disciplines:
Medical AI, radiology, clinical decision support systems, healthcare ethics, algorithmic bias

Part 5: Partnership

Direct Citations
1 Lång, K., et al. (2023). Artificial intelligence-supported screen reading versus standard double reading in the Mammography Screening with Artificial Intelligence trial (MASAI): A clinical safety analysis. The Lancet Oncology, 24(8), 936-944.
2 Rodríguez-Ruiz, A., et al. (2019). Stand-alone artificial intelligence for breast cancer detection in mammography: Comparison with 101 radiologists. Journal of the National Cancer Institute, 111(9), 916-922.

3 Freeman, K., et al. (2021). Use of artificial intelligence for image analysis in breast cancer screening programmes: Systematic review of test accuracy. British Medical Journal, 374, n1872.
4 Fenton, J. J., et al. (2007). Influence of computer-aided detection on performance of screening mammography. New England Journal of Medicine, 356(14), 1399-1409.
5 Jumper, J., et al. (2021). Highly accurate protein structure prediction with AlphaFold. Nature, 596, 583-589.
6 The Nobel Prize in Chemistry 2024. NobelPrize.org. Nobel Prize Outreach AB 2024.
7 Varadi, M., et al. (2022). AlphaFold Protein Structure Database: Massively expanding the structural coverage of protein-sequence space with high-accuracy models. Nucleic Acids Research, 50, D439-D444.
8 Lam, R., et al. (2023). GraphCast: Learning skillful medium-range global weather forecasting. Science, 382(6677), 1416-1421.
9 European Centre for Medium-Range Weather Forecasts. (2023). Storm Ciarán analysis and forecasting challenges. ECMWF.
10 California Independent System Operator. (2022). Post-Event Report: September 2022 Heat Storm. CAISO.
11 California Independent System Operator. (2022). Summer Loads and Resources Assessment. CAISO.
12 Denholm, P., Sun, Y., & Mai, T. (2019). An Introduction to Grid Services: Concepts, Technical Requirements, and Provision from Wind. National Renewable Energy Laboratory.
13 Bank of England & Financial Conduct Authority. (2024). Artificial Intelligence in UK Financial Services - 2024. Bank of England.
14 UK Finance. (2024). Annual Fraud Report 2024. UK Finance.
15 UK Finance. (2024). UK Payments Markets 2024 - Summary. UK Finance.
16 Pant, D., & Srivastava, P. (2022). Reducing false positives in bank anti-fraud systems based on rule induction in distributed tree-based models. Expert Systems with Applications, 189, 116094.
17 Da Silva Moore v. Publicis Groupe, 287 F.R.D. 182 (S.D.N.Y. 2012).
18 Angwin, J., Larson, J., Mattu, S., & Kirchner, L. (2016). Machine bias: Risk assessments in criminal sentencing. ProPublica.

19 VanLehn, K. (2011). The relative effectiveness of human tutoring, intelligent tutoring systems, and other tutoring systems. Educational Psychologist, 46(4), 197-221.
20 Khan Academy. (2023). Introducing Khanmigo for Individuals. Khan Academy Blog.
22 UNESCO. (2023). Guidance for generative AI in education and research. UNESCO.
23 Canuto, M.A., et al. (2018). Ancient lowland Maya complexity as revealed by airborne laser scanning of northern Guatemala. Science, 361(6409).
24 Chase, A.F., et al. (2012). Geospatial revolution and remote sensing LiDAR in Mesoamerican archaeology. Proceedings of the National Academy of Sciences, 109(32), 12916-12921.
25 PACUNAM. (2016-2018). LiDAR Survey of the Maya Biosphere Reserve. PACUNAM LiDAR Initiative.
26 SCAPE. (2019-2020). Scotland's Coastal and Inland Archaeological Mapping. SCAPE Trust.
27 Carroll, S.R., et al. (2020). The CARE Principles for Indigenous Data Governance. Data Science Journal, 19(43).
28 UNESCO. (2019). Operational Guidelines for the Implementation of the World Heritage Convention. UNESCO World Heritage Centre.
29 Willett, F.R., et al. (2021). High-performance brain-to-text communication via handwriting. Nature, 593, 249-254.
30 Pandarinath, C., et al. (2018). Inferring single-trial neural population dynamics using sequential auto-encoders. Nature Methods, 15, 805-815.
31 Hochberg, L.R., et al. (2012). Reach and grasp by people with tetraplegia using a neurally controlled robotic arm. Nature, 486, 372-375.
32 Sun, D., et al. (2022). Why 90% of clinical drug development fails and how to improve it. Acta Pharmaceutica Sinica B, 12(7), 3049-3062.
33 Breakthrough Initiatives. (2016). Breakthrough Listen. Retrieved from https://breakthroughinitiatives.org
34 NASA. (2025). NASA's tally of planets outside our solar system reaches 6,000. NASA Exoplanet Science Institute.
35 Ma, P., et al. (2023). The Breakthrough Listen Search for Intelligent Life. Nature Astronomy.

36 Shallue, C.J., & Vanderburg, A. (2018). Identifying exoplanets with deep learning: A five-planet resonant chain around Kepler-80 and an eighth planet around Kepler-90. The Astronomical Journal, 155(2), 94.
37 Hewish, A., et al. (1968). Observation of a Rapidly Pulsating Radio Source. Nature, 217, 709-713.

Supporting Research

Medical Partnership:

Core Research:

• Taylor-Phillips, S., & Stinton, C. (2022). Double reading in breast cancer screening: Considerations for policy-making. British Journal of Cancer, 127(2), 161-171.

Longevity Partnership:

Core Research:

• Tunyasuvunakool, K., et al. (2021). Highly accurate protein structure prediction for the human proteome. Nature, 596, 590-596.
• Thornton, J.M., Laskowski, R.A., & Borkakoti, N. (2021). AlphaFold heralds a data-driven revolution in biology and medicine. Nature Medicine, 27, 1666-1669.

Climate Partnership:

Core Research:

• Bi, K., et al. (2023). Accurate medium-range global weather forecasting with 3D neural networks. Nature, 619, 533-538.
• Pathak, J., et al. (2022). FourCastNet: A global data-driven high-resolution weather model using adaptive Fourier neural operators. arXiv.

Energy Partnership:

Core Research:

• National Renewable Energy Laboratory. (2023). Grid Integration of Battery Energy Storage Systems. NREL.

• Jenkins, K., et al. (2016). Energy justice: A conceptual review. Energy Research & Social Science, 14, 174-182.

Economic Partnership:

Core Research:

• Financial Ombudsman Service. (2025). Decision DRN-5681900. Financial Ombudsman Service.

• FCA. (2024). GC24/5: Authorised Push Payment Fraud. Financial Conduct Authority.

Justice Partnership:

Core Research:

• Pyrrho Investments Ltd v MWB Property Ltd 2016 EWHC 256 (Ch).

• Brown v BCA Trading Ltd 2016 EWHC 1464 (Ch).

• Grossman, M.R. & Cormack, G.V. (2013). Technology-assisted review in e-discovery. Journal of the Association for Information Science and Technology, 64(7), 1465-1472.

• Dressel, J. & Farid, H. (2018). The accuracy, fairness, and limits of predicting recidivism. Science Advances, 4(1).

Guidance Documents:

• EDRM. (2019). Technology Assisted Review (TAR) Guidelines. EDRM/Duke Bolch Judicial Institute.

• The Sedona Conference. (2023). TAR Case Law Primer, Second Edition. The Sedona Conference.

Education Partnership:

Core Research:

• Koedinger, K.R., & Corbett, A.T. (2006). Cognitive tutors: Technology bringing learning sciences to the classroom. In K. Sawyer (Ed.), The Cambridge handbook of the learning sciences.

• Ma, W., et al. (2014). Intelligent tutoring systems and learning outcomes: A meta-analysis. Journal of Educational Psychology, 106(4), 901-918.

• Reich, J., & Ruipérez-Valiente, J.A. (2019). The MOOC pivot. Science, 363(6423), 130-131.

Key Books:

• Reich, J. (2020). Failure to Disrupt: Why Technology Alone Can't Transform Education. Harvard University Press.

• Watters, A. (2021). Teaching Machines: The History of Personalized Learning. MIT Press.

ARCHAEOLOGICAL PARTNERSHIP:

Core Research:

• Garrison, T.G., et al. (2019). Recentering the rural: Lidar and articulated landscapes among the Maya. Journal of Anthropological Archaeology, 53, 133-146.

• Evans, D., et al. (2013). Uncovering archaeological landscapes at Angkor using lidar. Proceedings of the National Academy of Sciences, 110(31), 12595-12600.

Ethics and Indigenous Data Sovereignty:

• Nicholas, G., & Bannister, K. (2004). Copyrighting the past? Emerging intellectual property rights issues in archaeology. Current Anthropology, 45(3), 327-350.

• Atalay, S. (2012). Community-Based Archaeology: Research with, by, and for Indigenous and Local Communities. University of California Press.

MIND PARTNERSHIP:

Core Research:

• Chalmers, D.J. (1995). Facing up to the problem of consciousness. Journal of Consciousness Studies, 2(3), 200-219.

• Mullard, A. (2016). Parsing clinical success rates. Nature Reviews Drug Discovery, 15, 447.

Key Books:

• Koch, C. (2012). Consciousness: Confessions of a Romantic Reductionist. MIT Press.

• Churchland, P.S. (2013). Touching a Nerve: The Self as Brain. W.W. Norton.

COSMIC PARTNERSHIP:

Core Research:

• Worden, P., et al. (2017). The Breakthrough Initiatives. Acta Astronautica, 142, 3-10.
• Petigura, E.A., et al. (2013). Prevalence of Earth-size planets orbiting Sun-like stars. Proceedings of the National Academy of Sciences, 110(48), 19273-19278.
• Tarter, J. (2001). The Search for Extraterrestrial Intelligence. Annual Review of Astronomy and Astrophysics, 39, 511-548.
• Sheikh, S.Z., et al. (2021). Machine learning for SETI. Nature Astronomy, 5, 1148-1155.

Key Books:

• Vakoch, D.A., & Dowd, M.F. (Eds.). (2015). The Drake Equation. Cambridge University Press.
• Davies, P. (2010). The Eerie Silence. Houghton Mifflin Harcourt.

RESEARCH DISCIPLINES:

Medical imaging, radiology, oncology, structural biology, computational biology, meteorology, atmospheric physics, electrical engineering, grid operations, financial technology, fraud detection, legal technology, e-discovery, educational psychology, learning sciences, archaeology, remote sensing, computational neuroscience, brain-computer interfaces, radio astronomy, exoplanet science, astrobiology, machine learning, artificial intelligence in healthcare, energy systems, algorithmic fairness, AI ethics.

Part 6: Beyond Partnership

Direct Citations:

1 Silver, D., et al. (2016). Mastering the game of Go with deep neural networks and tree search. Nature, 529, 484-489.
1a Silver, D., et al. (2017). Mastering the game of Go without human knowledge. Nature, 550, 354-359.
2 Silver, D., et al. (2017). Mastering the game of Go without human knowledge. Nature

3 Krakovna, V., Gleave, A., & others (2022). Refining the sharp left turn threat model. AI Alignment Forum.
4 Hubinger, E., et al. (2024). Sleeper Agents: Training Deceptive LLMs that Persist Through Safety Training. arXiv:2401.05566. Anthropic.
5 UK Government (2023). The Bletchley Declaration by Countries Attending the AI Safety Summit, 1-2 November 2023. Gov.uk. https://www.gov.uk/government/publications/ai-safety-summit-2023-the-bletchley-declaration
6 European Union (2024). Regulation (EU) 2024/1689 of the European Parliament and of the Council on Artificial Intelligence (AI Act). Official Journal of the European Union, 12 July 2024.
7 UK Department for Science, Innovation and Technology (2023). Introducing the AI Safety Institute. Gov.uk; NIST (2024). U.S. AI Safety Institute Consortium. National Institute of Standards and Technology.
8 UK Government (2023). £100 million initial funding for Frontier AI Taskforce (evolved into AI Safety Institute). Gov.uk press release, 24 April 2023; U.S. Senate Commerce Committee (2024). $10 million initial appropriation for U.S. AI Safety Institute, plus $10 million TMF award (July 2024).
9 Microsoft FY2024 Q4 earnings ($13.9B cash capex for cloud/AI infrastructure); Alphabet/Google Q2 2024 earnings ($12-13B quarterly capex for AI servers/datacenters); Meta Q4 2024 earnings ($14.8B quarterly capex).
10 Unger, N., & McLean, M. (2025). An Open Door: AI Innovation in the Global South amid Geostrategic Competition. Center for Strategic & International Studies. Quote: "AI export controls ... are inherently porous."
11 Metz, C. (2016). The Sadness and Beauty of Watching Google's AI Play Go. WIRED. (Professional commentary on AlphaGo strategies)

Supporting Research:

Medical AI and Detection Systems:

• Wong, A., et al. (2021). External validation of sepsis prediction models. JAMA Network Open

Climate and Energy Systems:

• Schultz, M. G., et al. (2021). Can deep learning beat numerical weather prediction? Philosophical Transactions of the Royal Society A
• Brattle Group. (2024). Virtual power plants: Market potential and economic analysis
Financial Systems and Fraud Detection:
• UK Finance industry briefings on fraud prevention systems
• FCA reviews of automated decision-making in financial services
Drug Discovery and Structural Biology:
• Hassabis, D., & Jumper, J. (2024). AlphaFold and AI-driven scientific discovery. Nature Reviews
AI Safety and Governance:
• Bostrom, N. (2014). Superintelligence: Paths, dangers, strategies. Oxford University Press
• Carlsmith, J. (2022). Is power-seeking AI an existential risk? Open Philanthropy
• Various AI governance framework analyses

RESEARCH DISCIPLINES:
AI safety research, machine learning, medical imaging, clinical trials, climate modeling, weather forecasting, energy systems, grid operations, financial fraud detection, structural biology, drug discovery, international governance, risk assessment

Epilogue: A Personal Note from the Author

Direct Citations:

1 OECD.AI. (2024). AI Incidents and Controversies Database. Available at incidents.oecd.ai
2 Ministry of Industry and Information Technology & Ministry of Finance. (2025). National AI Industry Investment Fund (60 billion yuan / $8.2 billion). Announced January 2025. China Daily
3 Federal AI investment including: NITRD & National AI Initiative Office. (2024). Supplement to the President's FY2025 Budget: AI R&D investment ($3.3 billion). Released November 27, 2024; Department of Defense AI and autonomy programs ($13.4+ billion, FY2025)

4 European Commission. (2025). Policy target to mobilise €20 billion annually in combined public-private AI investment (AI policy page). Programme funding includes: Digital Europe Programme Work Programme 2025-2027 (€1.3 billion investment); Horizon Europe Digital call 2025 (€536.1 million budget)
5 AI Index Steering Committee. (2025). Artificial Intelligence Index Report 2025. Stanford Institute for Human-Centered AI, Stanford University
6 BigID. (2025). AI Risk & Readiness in the Enterprise — 2025 Report. Published June 2025
7 Shane, T. S. (2024). AI incident reporting: Addressing a gap in the UK's regulation of AI. Centre for Long-Term Resilience, December 2024
8 Hubinger, E., Denison, C., Mu, J., Lambert, M., Tong, M., Henighan, T., Herbert-Voss, A., Hubinger, E., ... Perez, E., et al. (2024). Sleeper Agents: Training Deceptive LLMs that Persist Through Safety Training. arXiv:2401.05566. Anthropic

INDEX

THE HUMAN THREAD

P

R

Printed in Dunstable, United Kingdom

73904531R00178